A Hot Mess:

How to Go From Being a Hot Mess to Happy Success

by Bo Bradley

The contents of this work, including, but not limited to, the accuracy of events, people, and places depicted; opinions expressed; permission to use previously published materials included; and any advice given or actions advocated are solely the responsibility of the author, who assumes all liability for said work and indemnifies the publisher against any claims stemming from publication of the work.

The information contained in this book is intended to be educational and not for diagnosis, prescription, or treatment of any health disorder whatsoever. This book is sold with the understanding that neither the author nor publisher is engaged in rendering any legal, psychological, or accounting advice. The publisher and author disclaim personal liability, directly or indirectly, for advice of information presented within. Although the author and publisher have prepared this manuscript with utmost care and diligence and have made every effort to ensure the accuracy and completeness of the information contained within, we assume no responsibility for errors, inaccuracies, omissions, or inconsistencies.

This book was researched and stories were gathered from various victims with their permission. It is a work of fiction. Any names, events, or places of similarity are purely coincidental.

All Rights Reserved
Copyright © 2016 by Bo Bradley

No part of this book may be reproduced or transmitted, downloaded, distributed, reverse engineered, or stored in or introduced into any information storage and retrieval system, in any form or by any means, including photocopying and recording, whether electronic or mechanical, now known or hereinafter invented without permission in writing from the publisher.

Dorrance Publishing Co
585 Alpha Drive
Pittsburgh, PA 15238
Visit our website at *www.dorrancebookstore.com*

ISBN: 978-1-4809-3570-9
eISBN: 978-1-4809-3547-1

CONTENTS

Introduction ix
Chapter 1—The "Aha Moment" 1
Chapter 2—My Move to Victimville .13
Chapter 3—Diving Deeper 23
Chapter 4—I Can't Even Die Right! .29
Chapter 5—Babies Having Babies 39
Chapter 6—This Is What I Deserve .51
Chapter 7—Desperate Love 57
Chapter 8—Rough Edges 69
Chapter 9—Revenge Is Sweet 75
Chapter 10—Codependent Mama 87
Chapter 11—Perpetuating Revenge .99
How to Turn a Hot Mess into a Happy Success 107
Chapter 12—The Codependent's Code 109
Chapter 13—Stop Being a Rescue Ranger 117
Chapter 14—Your Line in the Sand 123
Chapter 15—Zombie Before Zen 129
Chapter 16—Sweet Surrender 133
Chapter 17—Learning Healthy Love 141
Chapter 18—Get Your Revenge! 149
Author's Note 153
Resources 155

ACKNOWLEDGMENTS & DEDICATIONS

This book is dedicated to my mom—a woman of strength, loyalty, and faith. Thank you for being you. I am eternally grateful for the challenges and love you have gifted me within this life. I love you!

For my soul mate, my deceased husband, Dave. You brought me more joy and love than mere words can describe. I love you always, all-ways. Thank you for being my most active guardian angel.

For my twin flame, Guy. The word love is not enough to describe how I feel about you. I am ever grateful we found each other in this life. It is with great happiness and anticipation that I look forward to what the spirits have in store for us.

To my heart sister Cheri. Thank you for your time, insight, and wisdom in helping me tell this story.

A heartfelt thank you to Gail Shoop at Quintessence Photography for always making me look good. And to Erin Pace Molina for her awesome cover design. You rock.

"The absolute best revenge is to be happy ... and if you're truly happy, revenge no longer matters."

- Bo Bradley

INTRODUCTION

By all accounts, reason, and statistics, I should be dead—or at the very least, still a hot mess. The things I've seen, the things I've survived, no one should ever have to go through one of those experiences—let alone all of them.

To the outside world, I appeared to be a reasonably attractive, petite, polite, and quiet little girl. I lived with my average middle-class family in an average home located in your average neighborhood. I was the only girl, and the middle child. Even my name was average— Rebecca. Inside my world, which is the world you rarely share with others, I was ugly, unwanted, stupid, unlovable, and deserved every terrible thing that ever happened to me. I wasn't sure why I had even been born. What was the point of all this suffering? It seemed that no matter what I did, it was always wrong. I didn't fit in with my family. Both of my brothers are tall with blonde hair and blue eyes. I am short with mousy brown hair and hazel-green eyes. Sometimes my eyes look brown, sometimes green, sometimes just mixed up. I always thought you could tell my mood by what color my eyes appeared to be. My brothers' eyes were always just blue.

They looked like my parents. I didn't.

My brothers were loud, boisterous, normal boys. I was quiet and painfully shy, though people who know me today wouldn't believe it. I would whisper my answers to my teachers in school. I would quietly play by myself for hours. You could ask me for anything, and I would do it if I could. I loved to help. It was the one thing that made me feel good. I went through my younger years feeling as though I lived in a shell. I would picture it around me, protecting me from the harsh world. It was a soft golden color, yet surprisingly strong. It curled tightly around my body and rose up into the air. I could see out, but no one could see in. I could be invisible if I wanted, and I proved it often by how much others never seemed to notice me.

The only time I would rise out of my protective shell was when I saw someone hurting, someone unable to defend herself, or heard something that did not ring true in my heart. Then I would speak out. Then I would stand as tall as my tiny frame would allow. I would question. I would push back. It was almost as if I channeled an ancient warrior goddess. I felt no fear in those moments.

I would stand in front of the tallest, meanest bully and challenge him right back—if he was picking on anyone other than me. When the bullying was directed at me I never defended myself. The warrior goddess did not trouble herself for me. Others were more important than me. I didn't matter that much. I believed I didn't deserve to matter.

With the exception of those times I was helping someone or defending them, I felt like your basic "black sheep" of the family. They all loved going to the social gatherings at the church; I hated being stuck in the mass of people. I would rather be at home, in my room, reading. They all liked vegetables; I hated them. I was constantly scolded for not acting like a little lady; I was a tomboy and hated pink and dresses. The boys were revered. I never heard them get scolded the same way I got treated. One was Mom's favorite and one was Dad's favorite. I was just there—no one's favorite. I often had fantasies that I was adopted and that one day my real family would find me and rescue me from all of this.

And then there was my undying love affair with victimhood. I had come to believe that the whole world did it to and against me. I had no power to control my world. You know "Murphy's Law?" If anything bad can happen, it will—and to me. This became my life's motto. I believed I must have been Murphy in another life. I felt like I wasn't good enough for anything, and I was powerless to change it.

This pattern continuously played in my life, setting up a cycle of being a victim over and over. At this point, I felt like I had a disease. In my desperate search to find a "cure" for myself, I stumbled across the book, *Codependent No More* by Melody Beattie. From this book, I discovered I was codependent. Codependency felt like a disease. I felt like an alcoholic, except that love and the need to be needed were my drink.

When I felt like someone needed me to fix something for her and make her feel better, it was intoxicating. It temporarily made me feel good. It suppressed my nagging suspicions that I was worthless. When I was needed and fixed other people's problems, I felt powerful and high from the feeling of relief like I did have some use—truly a high much like an addict would feel with that next drink or dose of heroin.

When I have shared even part of my journey with someone, I have usually been met with disbelief.

"I don't believe you. Those things couldn't have happened to you. You don't act like it." And it is true. I don't act like it. My past behavior, the bad things I'm going to describe to you in this book, none of those things define who I am today.

Just for the record, my journey didn't start on a higher level or a desire to rise above anything. It actually all started with something much darker—a desire for revenge. Revenge for being a constant victim. Revenge for never being good enough.

So in my desire for revenge, I made some surprising discoveries—ones that completely changed my journey. Ones that asked me to dig deep and take a good hard, honest look at myself. It required an exploration of what role I was playing in my own perceived misery and suffering. I had to come to the realization that to stop uselessly blaming the world for all of my misfortunes—teen pregnancy, multiple marriages, untold emotional hardships—I had to, in a sense, go to "mental rehab." I had to quit thinking that life just happened to me. I had to take responsibility for my own life. But before you can take responsibility, you must first come to recognize some simple, true facts. Those facts—how I survived, and permanently broke the self-defeating pattern—are what you will find within these pages.

By sharing my own story, I hope you will be inspired to break your own self-defeating pattern. By sharing the tools I use to create my own happily-ever-after, I hope you will use them to create your own, changing your story to your own fairytale life. I wish you transformational success as you begin your journey, hopefully with fresh insight and ideas to make your life better.

My version of this story starts at the pivotal point—the point where it all began to truly change. Just know this as you dive in, my friend: I would not change one thing that has happened on my journey.

CHAPTER 1

THE "AHA!" MOMENT

I sat on the hard asphalt of the school yard, hiding within the evening shadows behind a trash can, my heart racing as I tried to catch my breath and think; *just think, damn it!* While I waited for my breath to slow, I peered out to the street, looking for his car to drive by. Was he out looking for me? Did he wonder why I ran off like a maniac? The argument that had driven me to run faded to the background as other thoughts took over. Different scenarios of what would happen if he found me ran through my mind.

My mind showed me these scenarios as if they were mini-movies. I watched as he found me and choked the life out of me. I watched as he just pointed and laughed at my attempt at hiding from him. I watched as he raised his big hands and swung them at my tear-stained face. I watched as he cried and begged for my forgiveness. I watched as he caught me in his arms, kissed me, and told me how much he needed me. I watched as he told me everything I wanted to hear. I watched as I kept on running, never stopping, abandoning my family and friends to survive. I watched as I slit my own wrists and silently bled out. I watched as I swallowed too many pills and drifted into oblivion. I watched as I sat there, waiting for him to look for me—and he never did.

Not in one single mini-movie did I straighten my spine and do what my gut was screaming at me. Why? I had married this man. I had let myself get carried away in the whirlwind romance.

I had met Mark just a little over a year after my divorce from Jack was final. I had been out to the local country bar with my girlfriends. We were dancing, laughing, and having a great time. My friend Teresa had just challenged me to my favorite game, "That Guy."

"That Guy" was a game we had made up. One of us would pick out a guy from across the bar, one that we thought was good looking but who wasn't paying attention to us. The challenged girl had to get him to talk to her without saying a word to him. The rules included no going after a guy who was with a girl, no sending notes, and no talking to his buddies to get him over to you. It was a game I usually won.

"That guy," Teresa said, pointing to a tall man with dark hair, a mustache, and what looked like blue eyes standing next to the DJ booth. With tight jeans, a beer in his hand, and a black cowboy hat slightly tilted back, he looked like your quintessential urban cowboy. "You're on," I said, thinking I was going to enjoy this. He was really good looking.

I made my way through the crowd, getting closer. I took a deep breath and allowed my smile to light my face. As I sauntered past this particular cowboy, I counted on the crowd to press me closer. As it did, I looked directly into his eyes and telepathically sent him a message: "Follow me!" From the corner of my eye, I saw his head swivel and follow my movement through the people.

I waited at the bar with my back to where he had stood. With a secret grin I ordered my drink and felt him move up behind me. "I'll get that," he offered in a deep, sexy voice. I took my drink and turned around to thank him. Wow! He was even better looking up close. "Thank you, Teresa," I said in my mind as he introduced himself.

His name was Mark, and he had me instantly charmed. He acted as though I was the only woman in the world and all he wanted to do was take care of me. Proof that this was true, or so I thought, came later that evening.

While I was busy being charmed by Mark, a guy who had previously bothered Teresa showed up. She had made it clear to this guy on several occasions that she was not interested. It didn't seem to stop him from persisting, as though he could wear her down.

So wrapped up with Mark, I hadn't seen him enter the bar. Our other friend knew she had to let me know that trouble was brewing. She immediately grabbed my attention when she squeezed between Mark and me and said, "The pest is back." Knowing that the presence of this guy would cause Teresa to become upset, I apologized to Mark and told him I would talk to him later. I had to rescue my friend. As I hurried toward Teresa, I saw that the guy had her backed into a corner. "Come on, sweet thang," he said as he loomed over my friend, "you know you want to know me."

Fear, anger, and disgust warred on her face. Her eyes met my own as I got closer, and seemed to scream to me, "Help me!"

With no other thought than to rescue my friend, I reached up and grabbed the pest's shoulder, spinning him to face me. My words came out low, clipped, and forceful. I could feel the anger burn my face red as I said, "You! Pest! You've been told to leave her alone. Back the fuck away from her now."

"It's a free country, bitch. I can talk to whomever I want!" He smirked.

"Then you're going to have to go through me," I snarled back. I took a step toward him, all of my five foot one frame ready to prove my point. A pair of strong arms wrapped around me, gently restraining me.

I glanced up and my eyes found Mark's. He winked at me and then told the pest, "I think you'd better leave now, pal. I can't keep holding her back—and when she's done, I'll step in. Now stop bothering my friends and leave."

The pest looked up at Mark, six foot one with a strong build, and quickly decided it wasn't worth it. He left the bar and found someone else to pester, I'm sure.

From that moment, Mark represented hope to me. Hope that I no longer had to be in charge of everything. Hope that someone would rescue me for a change. Hope that I could actually rely on and trust in someone. Hope that I would, at last, be loved.

Within weeks, Mark had moved in with me and proposed marriage, which I swiftly accepted. He had charmed my family and friends and swept me away in a whirlwind of romance. Little things had cropped up here and there, like a quick temper, stories that didn't add up, and money disappearing. But they were all explained and soothed away. After all, they were just little things, right?

I just knew that with a little encouragement, he would become a strong, successful man—and we would live happily ever after. I could help him fix those areas in his life where he stumbled. He would love me for it. We were married within months.

Over the next two years, the irresponsible behaviors, temper tantrums, and all those little things grew larger and larger, increasing in frequency. It had become the norm. It was just how it was. I didn't realize how bad it had gotten. He never got physically violent, but he talked about it. He talked about using his gun in the military. He talked about how it felt when he had to kill. It seemed as if some part of him thrilled at the thought, though he never came out and said it.

Back at my hiding spot on the playground, reality had set in.

Reality was that I was exhausted. Exhausted from running, exhausted from my life. When had I become the victim again? Was I really just a gutless wonder? I was so tired of all the trauma drama. I wanted to be that person who was hidden deep inside me, the one I rarely let see the light of day. But how?

I knew I had some decisions to make. Important decisions. Life-changing decisions. Decisions that would not only affect me, but my children as well. Could I make the right ones this time?

"Probably not. You've screwed it up time and time again. What makes you think you can do anything different this time?" the cynical critic in my head yelled at me. Feelings of shame, guilt, and worthlessness washed over me. I just wanted to run away and be rescued by someone. Lou! He'd rescue me. He'd take me away from all of this. He told me to call him if I ever needed him.

Lou was my friend, my confidante. We worked together, looked out for each other, and carried a deep respect for each other. A part of me was in love with him. Another part of me knew we would never be more than friends and love each other as such.

As I began to dial the phone, I practiced what I would say. Tears were rolling down my face, and then I found my finger hanging suspended over that last button. "No," my broken voice whispered. I swore I would never be or act like a victim again, and yet wasn't that just what I doing?

I was blaming the events of my past, wanting someone to come fix it for me, and helping me avoid choices and consequences. Hiding from a manipulative man at a school playground like a scared little kid, while my own three kids were probably wondering where Mommy was at. What on earth was I doing?

That creeping, shameful feeling that had washed over me was because I knew what I had done. I had fallen right back into my old pattern of codependence. I had grown comfortable over the years, allowed my desperate need to be good enough and to be loved make my decisions once again.

Years before, when I was in the midst of my divorce from my first husband Jack, I had read *Codependent No More* by Melody Beattie. I recognized then that I was codependent and had sworn that would change. Through that book I gained great insight and temporary strength that allowed me to stand by my decision to divorce Jack. Even though I had two children and was pregnant with my third, I knew I was better off as a single mother than to stay married to a man with who I felt like more of a mother to than a wife. I had followed the prescribed "twelve steps" and thought I was cured.

My second marriage would be different, I vowed. It could be saved. I would no longer tolerate his lies, his possessiveness. I would hold my boundaries and—but wait—what were my boundaries? I couldn't define my boundaries to save my life. I couldn't tell you what I wanted. I was only beginning to know what I didn't want.

Knowing I wasn't quite ready to make any big decisions, yet feeling more anchored in my body, I stood up and brushed the dirt from my jeans. With a swipe at my tears and a few deep breaths, I slowly began to walk toward home. Better—but still ignoring what my gut was screaming at me to do. I wasn't ready to hear it yet.

Walking through the door of our home was like an out-of-body experience. The activities going on inside were the same as they had been over the last few years, but I was different. I felt different. The kids were watching TV, and Mark was sprawled in the corner of our couch like nothing had happened two hours ago. They immediately let me know they were hungry for dinner. Meeting Mark's eyes briefly, I walked to the kitchen to prepare dinner. I was looking for a spark, a glimpse of hope that it really could be different. I just felt numb.

The kids were laughing and talking, with Mark occasionally joining in. I felt as if I stood outside it all, observing, assessing. My body moved on autopilot, while my mind was busy categorizing how I would discuss what I was feeling with Mark, my husband.

After we finished eating dinner—and the kids were in bed—I sat next to Mark on the couch, ready to talk. He was once again zoning out on the TV. I turned it off. He looked at me, waiting for my apology for running off—and this would have been my usual pattern. Get mad. Confront Mark. Get scared—scared that he would lose control and hit me. Scared that he would leave me. Apologize. Act as if nothing had happened.

This time, I caught myself before the words, "I'm sorry," came out of my mouth. I wasn't sorry. I was tired. I was in pain. I was still scared. But I was determined. Determined to do it differently. I took a deep breath and grounded myself.

"Things have got to change with us, Mark. I married you to be my partner, to share the responsibilities. I married you because I trusted you and I loved you. But I'm tired, Mark. I'm tired of always taking the reins. I'm tired of always being the heavy. I'm tired of making all the decisions. I'm just tired of trying to do it all. I need your help."

He reached over and patted my knee. "I understand. I'll do whatever you want. What can I do to make it better?"

Where do I start? To Mark I said, "Stop taking money from the bank just because it says we have it. That money is for bills. Just check with me if you need money. Help me out with the kids. Sometimes you have to be the one to say 'no' to them."

"I can do that," he said. "Anything else?"

Taking a breath, I brought up the one thing that had really gotten bad: his lying. "Yes. Please always be honest with me. I'm so tired of all the lying. For God's sake, the last time you lied to me about a coupon!"

"I was afraid you'd get mad." he said.

"I get mad when you lie, so that defeats your purpose, doesn't it?" I fired back.

Holding his hands up in defense, he said, "OK. OK. I see your point. Let's not get into that again. I'll tell you the truth, even if I think you'll get mad." He told me everything I wanted to hear, yet why did I still feel numb? I went to bed, wondering what tomorrow would bring, wishing I could believe his words.

Over the next several months, things did change. Our relationship got worse. The house was like a minefield. The tension affected everyone, yet we took care to make sure the face we presented to the outside world made it appear as if everything was wonderful.

In the privacy of home I began experiencing "funks" more frequently. My funks consisted of not showering, barely eating, and getting no enjoyment out of anything. I wouldn't even read, one of my favorite pastimes. Either I would go to work, faking normalcy, or I would call in sick.

Whether I faked it at work or not, when I was at home I'd sit with the shades drawn, in the shadows, and pick my life apart. I'd allow my inner critic free rein in my mind. My critic would proceed to point out every one of my flaws and why I was so unlovable.

"You're stupid. You're fat. You're ugly. No one could really love you. You can't do anything right." And so on. This would continue until that part of me I had buried so deep would say *"Enough!"* Then the cycle would start all over again.

Before, Mark would occasionally call to check where I was when I was away from the house. I never understood this, because I had always told him where I was going. Now, he would call me within minutes of my leaving the house. He questioned where I was, whom I was with, and what I was doing. He was acting as if I was having an affair. I felt like I couldn't breathe. I was constantly under scrutiny.

When I'd get home from work he'd grill me on what job sites I had gone to, who I had talked to. He began accusing me outright of cheating. I asked him where in the world he thought I was doing this while at work—in the blue room? Blue rooms were what we called the portable toilets on the job.

"You have that van." he yelled, as if this was the most obvious thing in the world. He was talking about my work van, which I used to go from job site to job site, conducting safety inspections and training.

I couldn't help myself. I snorted and gave a sarcastic reply. "Oh, yeah. You caught me. The superintendents let me come onto the job and pick which guy I want to do for the day. I don't actually do anything else. They pay me to fuck all day."

Realizing how ridiculous it sounded when stated so blatantly, and that he couldn't twist the reality around to keep the focus off himself, he stormed off. His behavior continued to become more and more erratic, and intolerable.

One time, I left the house to go to an appointment, leaving Mark to watch the kids. Five minutes down the road I realized I had forgotten something. I turned around to go back when I saw him driving away through the neighborhood. He had left my three children in the house, alone. They were only three, four, and nine years old.

As I waited for him to return home, my appointment now missed, I wondered how many times over the last few years he had done this. How often had my kids been in danger? How could I not know this had been happening? I was beyond angry—angry with him and angry with myself.

My anger began to turn even further inward. I heard my old friend the critic rise to the occasion. *See? You're such a lousy mother. You left your kids with an irresponsible idiot that YOU married. If one of them had been hurt, it would have been all your fault.*

Hours later, waiting with my arms crossed and fists clenched, still feeling shame and guilt, I lashed out at him before he made it in the door. "Where the hell were you?" I screamed with the fearlessness of a mother bear protecting her cubs. "You left our kids completely alone. What the hell were you thinking? I trusted you to watch them."

Mark looked at me with nonchalance. His fighter was nowhere to be found. "So what?" he replied with an indifference that left my stomach churning. "Nothing happened to them," he said with the same apathy.

"Ben's old enough to watch the younger ones."

"He's only nine," I shouted back, feeling indignant. This was met with a shoulder shrug from Mark. I shook my head in disgust and said, "I obviously made a mistake in trusting you with my children."

He just said, "Whatever," and plopped down in his usual spot on the couch, turning on the TV.

Stunned by his apathetic response, I gave up the argument. It was pointless. I was too tired to fight someone who obviously didn't even care. I felt the terrible weight of fatigue settle in on my brain. Feeling defeated, I walked to the bedroom in the back, the bland-colored room with the cheap laminated black-and-gold furniture and bright red comforter on the queen-sized bed. It seemed lifeless to me now. I sat down on it, forlorn but contemplative. How could this go on? The weight of anger, sadness, angst, and depression was so heavy that my shoulders ached. The voice lit up inside of my head. All the dark criticism I heaped on myself felt like a bulldozer running over my head.

The old litany of degradation and self-criticism returned. *You're an idiot. You're a fool. What are you going to do? How can someone like you raise three children? This man couldn't love someone as stupid and low as you are. No one could. You deserve it. You're a failure at everything. No one will ever want you. You will never be good enough. This is all you will ever get. When will you learn?*

And the more the self-loathing continued, the more the fatigue set in. I wanted to close my eyes and sink into dark oblivion. I wanted the voices to turn off. I wanted to feel anything but so low and depressed.

After dragging myself off to work the next day, I realized it was time to prepare for the drug awareness training I would be conducting. As I went over the signs and symptoms of drug use, I automatically began checking off the symptoms as they pertained to Mark:

- Becomes disrespectful—is verbally or physically abusive—Mark, check.
- Is angry a lot, acts paranoid, suffers from extreme mood swings—Mark, check.
- Is secretive and lies about what he doing and where he is going—Mark, check.

- Seems apathetic in situations more than usual—Mark, check.
- Is stealing or losing possessions—Mark, check.
- Seems to have a lot of money or is always asking for money—Mark, check.
- Withdrawn from activities he used to enjoy—Mark, check.
- Not taking care of hygiene and grooming—Mark, check.
- Not sleeping, or sleeping too much—I was unsure of this one, because I went to bed and then left for work before he did.
- Loss of appetite—his appetite appeared fine.
- Weight loss or gain—Mark, check.
- Too hyperactive or too little energy—Mark, check.
- Loses concentration and is having trouble remembering things—Mark, check.
- Irritability—Mark, check.
- Impulsive behavior—Mark, check.
- Aggressiveness—Mark, check.

He fit almost every one. Was it possible? Was my husband using drugs on top of everything else? Stunned and not wanting to believe it, I tried to look for other ways to explain his recent behavior. Nothing came to mind.

In my gut I knew the truth. My body chilled and began to shake as I realized this was a deal breaker for me. It was over. I knew I could not live with a drug abuser. It explained the disappearing money, the lies, the erratic behavior, Mark's sudden disappearances, and so much more.

I also knew that someone on drugs could become very violent. He was a big man at six foot one. I was only five foot one and had my children to think of. I couldn't imagine him physically hurting the kids, yet the picture of him using his shotgun on me was frightfully clear. His ever-increasing violent talk worried me. He had told me he had killed people while in the military. He talked frequently of how he would "take someone out" who betrayed him. I could see him shooting me without any thought. I knew I had to do something quickly to make it as safe as possible for everyone.

That evening, while Mark had disappeared somewhere, I called my dad, a highway patrolman. I felt sure he would understand and help me. I explained what had been going on over the last several months. I ticked off all the symptoms of drug abuse he was displaying. I asked my dad to come get Mark's shotgun from the house. I expressed my fears.

Instead of the support I had hoped for, my dad asked, "Don't you think you're exaggerating? I don't think it's necessary to come get the gun. He wouldn't hurt you." Dad had stuck a knife in my already-wounded heart.

Mark had charisma. People loved him instantly. He could charm almost anyone. In hindsight, I noticed that after people really got to know him, they had little to do with him. But when I made the phone call, my dad was still charmed by Mark.

My dad eventually came to get the gun, but only because I was so insistent.

The time had come. I had talked to Lou and had him on standby to come over if I needed him or felt like I was in danger. After making sure the kids were out of the house and wouldn't be back for several hours, I approached Mark.

"Mark, we need to talk," I said with trepidation but with a confidence I gained by holding the phone in my hand, finger ready to push the "Lou" panic button.

"About what?" he railed with irritation. "What do you think I did wrong now?" My stomach twisted in agonizing fear. I felt cold to the bone, even though it was ninety-eight degrees outside. It was now or never. "I want a divorce," I said with a flat determination.

"What's with the phone?" he snarled as he clenched his fists. "You going to call your lover, Lou?"

This response didn't come unexpected. "No," I replied with confidence. "I've told you that Lou isn't my lover. This isn't about Lou, anyway. It never has been."

"Prove it," he yelled. "Prove that you're not having an affair."

"What?" I said, "How can I prove that? I have never cheated on you or anyone else. That is not who I am! Lou and I are friends. But if that's what it takes for you to get out of here, believe whatever you want."

He turned away from me. "Don't bother looking for your gun. I had my dad take it from the house. You'll get it back when I feel safe again."

My comment stopped him in his tracks. He had been heading back to the bedroom. With narrowed eyes he stared at me for a moment, and then he changed tactics. He softened his stance. Tears were in his eyes as he said, "So where am I supposed to go?"

The rescuer in me immediately wanted to fix it for him. Pulling in every ounce of strength I could muster, I said, "I don't care. Just not here."

I waited in the living room, the phone still cradled in my hand, as he packed some bags and then left to go wherever. With relief, I felt my shoulders drop as I called Lou to let him know that Mark had left and I was alright.

Not until weeks later did I would learn where he went that night and ended up staying for almost a year. It would bring me betrayal in more ways than one.

CHAPTER 2

MY MOVE TO "VICTIMVILLE"

Betrayal hurt. It made me question everything again. It made me angry. I felt abandoned. I felt alone. I felt like I was so unlovable that even my flesh and blood, my parents, couldn't love me.

How else could you explain why they took Mark in? Yes, my parents brought the man I was afraid of, the one I knew was doing drugs, and the one who was a pathological liar, into their home. They thought I was wrong for kicking him out. That something was wrong with me—that I was making stuff up. What I said couldn't possibly be true, and I must be the one having an affair.

I was so raw, so bloodied inside, that in order to survive, I shut my feelings down. I survived through work and my kids. I moved through most days on autopilot. I made sure the divorce papers were filed.

I was relieved he was out of my home, away from my kids, yet I was embarrassed that my own family had chosen him over me. At least that's what it felt like.

I felt so lost. I didn't know how my life had gotten this way. I was now a two-time divorcee, bankrupted and with three children. Yes, now that he was gone I finally got to the truth of the finances that I could never seem to straighten out.

I had thought that it was my math skills. Math was not my best subject, but I had never thought that I was that horrible at it. Yet the checkbook never seemed to balance, and money that I thought we had would seem to disappear.

I was always juggling bills and trying to keep everyone fed. I made a decent paycheck, and so did Mark, so this never made sense to me.

I found I was so far in debt that it seemed my only way to survive was to file for bankruptcy. Every credit card had been maxed out. The savings was gone, and all the money put in the checking account to pay the bills was gone. I would have to let the house foreclose and find somewhere for my three children and me to live. I certainly couldn't ask my parents for help.

Feeling that bone-deep weariness that comes from defeat, I slumped onto the couch. As I looked around our dingy living room, it was blurred and softened by the tears in my eyes. The tears hid the cobwebs high in corners and seemed to blur the dirt on the walls, making it look as though it had been painted a dull off-white. The cheap posters in picture frames covered in dust made me wish for better times.

"It all has to go," I said to the empty room with my voice echoing off the dingy walls. I would have to pack it all up.

Just me. No one to help me. How would I ever get it all moved without help? I'd have to do what I hated doing. I'd have to ask friends to help me. It was the only solution my tired brain could see.

I let Mark know that the house would be going into foreclosure, unless he wanted to save it. I knew he would tell my parents this—and the hope that they would realize that I needed help lingered. No return call came.

It was just one more betrayal to me. Was this what my life would always be like? Would I always be the victim? The one left hurting? The one stepped on? When would it be my turn to have some peace, some happiness that lasted longer than an eye blink? What did I ever do to deserve this misery? In my heart, I believed I was a good person. I went out of my way to help everyone I could. When would someone finally help me?

In another desperate search for answers, I stumbled on the book, *Men are from Mars and Women are from Venus* by John Gray, Ph.D. Someone had turned on a light at the top of the deep well I had fallen into. It morphed from a pinprick to a softball-sized glow. That book began my journey of understanding myself, and why I was codependent; why I fell for the same type of guy over and over; why I was a perpetual victim. And it did one more thing—it gave me hope that I could change it.

What I had discovered was that before I could even try to understand anyone else, I needed to understand who I was as a person. Who I wanted to be. Why I had survived and experienced all that I had. What kind of friend I was.

What kind of friend I wanted. What my values and boundaries were. What would fulfill me? What were my gifts? What was I worth? What did I like and not like about me?

To learn these things, I would have to ruthlessly explore my past, look at old traumatic events that I thought I had buried away forever, open old wounds, shine the light on my shadows, and be brutally honest with myself.

The first old wound I examined was one that I rarely spoke about. I could count on one hand the number of people who knew about the wound. I had tried to forget it. I had tried to let go, but mostly, I just ignored it. I was determined to not let what had happened run my life. I started there because it was another time when those who were supposed to love me no matter what had betrayed me. That old wound was the first time I could recall truly feeling like a victim.

I was nine. I was fairly shy and small for my age. I remember lapping up attention wherever I could get it. For some reason, I never felt like I had enough attention. I didn't act out much, other than occasionally talking back or voicing my opinion when it perhaps would have been better if I hadn't. For the most part I was quiet, reading and writing a lot.

We were going to visit my grandparents. At my age it was a long trip, though in reality, the trip was only four hours from San Luis Obispo to Richmond, California, yet I was excited to go. Other than having to deal with my brothers in such close proximity, I enjoyed car rides. I liked to watch the scenery zip past as my dad sped along. The rhythm of the tires on the asphalt was soothing music to my ears. Watching the land morph from small town structures and beaches to tall city buildings fascinated me.

Content, yet tired from the long car ride, and happy to have arrived, I eagerly followed my parents up the driveway to knock on my grandparents' door. A short woman with steel gray hair and twinkling blue eyes answered the door—my grandma. A smile lit her face as she greeted each of us.

As I entered my grandparents' home, I inhaled deeply and took in scents of beans baking on the stove, cornbread cooking in the oven, and tobacco from grandpa's pipe wafting through it all. Ah! The smell of my grandparents' home. Gradually, the noise of more people began to filter into my ears, and I looked around and saw that most of my cousins had arrived before us. They were scattered around the living room, taking up chairs and areas of the floor, laughing and talking loudly. My grandpa sat like a king in his old black recliner, puffing quietly on his pipe, watching over his family.

The cousins, all older than I, fell into playing games with each other. The adults gathered around and shared stories about what they had been up to since they last saw each other. I watched it all, sitting quietly in a corner, alternately reading my book and listening to them tease and egg each other on.

After dinner I helped with the dishes while the other kids went outside to play and stretch their legs. It was expected of me to stick around the adults, as I was too young to hang out with the older kids. Once this chore was done, I found my way onto my grandpa's lap. I was tired and content to just sit there. He didn't say anything. He just gave me a squeeze and settled back in his recliner with his arms around me. After a few minutes he began to rub my tummy in small slow circles. His roughened fingers felt good on my soft skin, like a gentle scratch that was soothing. That gentle scratching soon lulled me into feeling sleepy.

I was starting to drift into sleep when something startled me fully awake. Grandpa shifted in his chair and suddenly something hard was poking into the small of my back. I shifted around thinking it was his belt buckle. His slow circles on my stomach had begun to get bigger while I was drifting, his hands getting ever closer to areas that made me feel uncomfortable. Areas that no one but me should be touching.

I sat up straighter, trying to relieve the poking in my back. Should I say something? Was I just being silly? Then his fingers brushed my newly budding breasts, circling down and slightly dipping under the elastic of my panties. I looked quickly at my parents. Did they see? What was happening? I felt strange.

Emotionally it felt heavy to me, wrong in a way I couldn't define. I blocked his fingers with my arms, thinking maybe he just wasn't aware where his fingers were brushing on me. Instead, his hands pushed hard against my arms. Not hard enough to bring attention to us, but enough to let me know it wasn't an accident. This was my grandpa. He wouldn't hurt me, would he? He wasn't hurting me physically, but it felt wrong just the same.

As the survivor in me surfaced, I knew I needed to escape. I said I needed to go to the bathroom and scrambled off his lap. As I stared blankly into the mirror, wondering what had just happened, I heard the critic voice in my head, *"You caused this, you know. You must have done something that made him think it was OK. I mean, he did it right in front of your parents' faces. There is something seriously wrong with you!"*

My face stained red as I fought back the tears of shame. *I can fix this! I'll stay away from him. I'll be even quieter, so everyone will forget I'm here.* I'd played invisible many times before, and for me it was a way to avoid. It also reinforced to me that I wasn't worth noticing.

I splashed cool water on my face to ease the red away and slipped silently out of the bathroom. I found a quiet corner and curled up with my book, pretending I hadn't seen him pat his lap, inviting me back.

That night my older brother and I slept in our sleeping bags on the living room floor of the house that I no longer considered cozy. The smell of leftover beans combined with the tobacco from Grandpa's pipe now turned my stomach. I was fearful but somewhat comforted to know that my brother was nearby. Somewhat fitfully I drifted off to sleep.

I woke very early the next morning. No one else was awake yet. I had woken because I was cold. Why was I so cold? Awareness came to me as a shock.

I was practically naked inside my sleeping bag. How had that happened? My eyes focused on my purple pajama top crumbled on the floor, inside out. How had that gotten there? Turning to look for my matching pajama bottoms, I realized they were twisted around my ankles. What had happened? As I turned back, I felt the cold air chill my body. The zipper was completely down on my sleeping bag.

Confused at how I had ended up in this state in my sleep, I turned my top right-side out and put it back on. I untangled my bottoms and pulled them up before anyone could see me this way. I scrunched down as deep as I could go within my sleeping bag. I didn't know what had happened to me. I didn't want to know. I was confused. I was scared by what it could mean. Instead, I willed myself back to sleep where I vowed I would forget this had ever happened. It was just a bad dream.

The mind is a powerful thing. I would not remember this event until I was eighteen and another attack brought it all back. Until then, I never told anyone what had happened. Yet I changed that night.

I became desperate to be in control; control of my feelings, control of everything around me. Inside I was feeling as if I was spiraling out of control. I stopped being so quiet. I would mouth off to anyone who said something I didn't like. I would smart off to my mom with increasing frequency. I took everything personally and blew it all out of proportion.

One night at dinner, as I was helping myself to seconds of mashed potatoes, one of my favorites, my dad said, "Do you really need that?" I looked at him, spoon suspended over my plate where I had just dumped those potatoes;

silently I questioned his statement. I didn't have the nerve to use my newly developed smart mouth to him.

"You're getting fat. You might want to watch how much you're eating," he said with an air of nonchalance as he continued to finish the food on his own plate. Stung, I let the spoon clatter onto my plate as I pushed away from the table. I looked to my mom, some part of me hoping she would rise to my defense. Through salty tears now running down my face, I saw her lips compress together. No defense would be coming from that sealed mouth.

I blindly ran to my room, slamming my door. Shutting them out. Shutting me in. I threw myself face down on the old twin bed, springs squeaking as my body landed. I grabbed my pillow and screamed my pain into it. Why had he said that? Was I really fat? Did my own dad hate me so much? I knew I had gotten a little bigger, but it hadn't seemed all that much. I flipped over and lifted my shirt, staring at my softly rounded tummy.

"Gross! Look at that. You are fat! No wonder no one likes you. Right now they're probably laughing at how fat you are." Disgusted with myself, I dropped my shirt and stared at the ceiling.

The self-loathing continued in my head. *So now you're not only stupid and worthless, you're fat. No one even wants to look at you. The one thing you had going for you was being skinny, and you blew that. What are you going to do about it now, fatso?*

"I'll stop eating." I grimly answered back.

Sure ya will, chubbs, was the snide retort.

This was the beginning of my slide into anorexia.

Under my mother's watchful eye, the next morning instead of my usual bowl of cereal and a slice of peanut butter toast, I ate only the toast. It tasted like ash in my mouth. Food was now my enemy. Satisfied that I had eaten something, my mother continued packing our lunches. I knew I had to be careful. I intended to eat as little as possible while making it look like I was eating normally.

I knew that if my mom suspected I wasn't eating, she would be afraid that it would look bad to others. She drilled in my head that we must keep up appearances, and to keep the pretense, I took the lunch she had made, but I never ate it.

At dinner, I took small spoonfuls of each item and then spread them about my plate, making it appear fuller than it actually was. I disciplined myself to eat very slowly, one piece at a time. I had discovered that eating very slowly and taking minuscule bites, which I chewed until there was nothing left, made me the last one at the table. After others left the room, I'd toss the rest of my food in the garbage disposal.

I never felt hungry anymore. I had convinced myself that all food tasted horrible, and so it did.

Every day I shut myself in the bathroom and inspected my body. As I looked in the mirror, I'd recite all that was wrong with me. "Look at that fat stomach. Yuck! No boobs and a fat stomach, aren't you just ugly. No boy is ever going to be attracted to you. Your own dad thinks you're ugly. You even have a fat face."

It didn't seem to matter that my clothes began to hang on my body like rags or that my belts were now at the tightest notch. I still saw the same fat, ugly girl in the mirror. I still heard the echo of my dad saying, "You're fat," over and over. No one had commented on my weight again; therefore, I concluded that I still must be fat and they'd just given up on me.

It seemed that the skinnier I got, the angrier I got. I stopped answering calls from friends. I spent more and more time alone in my room. I poured my heart and pain into poetry and stories. Every poem was heartbreaking, every story ending in tragedy.

During the outpouring of pain on paper, I had a vision of a tattoo. This was a tattoo that I knew was mine. I would one day have it, I vowed. Not only did my parents hate tattoos, which secretly thrilled me, but this tattoo represented what I believed my tragic destiny was. It was all I thought I deserved—though I couldn't tell you why.

I drew it wherever I could. Scribbled onto scraps of paper, in the corners of poems I penned. A heart with a lightning bolt and three drops of blood coming from the lightning wound. A sign of my perpetual broken heart. This was my fate. Happiness and love were not mine to claim. I was the bridge to get others to what their fate was. Nothing more.

Every boy I ever had a crush on was represented in that tattoo. Every person who ever made fun of me, every time I felt unwanted, worthless—it was all represented. That tattoo would hold all my pain, and my secret fears of never being enough, never being loved. It represented who I thought I was meant to be. I was twenty-one when I finally got the tattoo inked on the inside of my left ankle. The vision of it had stayed with me for all of the years in-between, and I gave in to it after my divorce from Jack.

Having decided that my destiny would forever be full of pain and angst, I no longer felt the need to try to be liked. I began to refuse, to make other plans—anything to get out of spending time with family or friends, especially going to my grandparents'. My family and friends didn't understand what was wrong with me. I couldn't explain it—to them or myself. I just knew that everything within me did not want to be there.

Eventually, my mom caught on to my poor eating habits. She took me to see the doctor. "She's not eating, and I don't know why," my mom told him as he began his examination of my rail-thin body. The doctor looked into my eyes and asked, "Are you eating?"

"I eat." I said with a shoulder shrug.

"Tell me what you eat."

"Sandwiches, dinner stuff, whatever."

"Do you eat a plateful, half a plate, or how much?"

"I eat some. I'm just not hungry."

The doctor and my mom exchanged glances. He finished his exam with the cold stethoscope on my scrawny chest where my ribs poked through. He then asked my mom to step out with him while I dressed. When they returned to the room, the doctor was holding a long needle.

I hated needles. They hurt. Looking at the needle with wide eyes, I asked, "What is that for?"

"This is what you will get if you do not start eating complete meals right away."

"Why? I'm not sick."

"You're well on your way to being sick. You're dehydrated and malnourished. You must eat or I will do this."

"Alright. Fine. I'll eat till I'm a fat pig again."

My mom released a heavy sigh at those words, but only said to the doctor, "I'll make sure she eats better. I'll monitor every bite if I have to."

Crap! This was going to be tough to keep the weight off now. I had gotten down to seventy-eight pounds and was starting to feel as though I might be considered thin.

My mind raced as I tried to come up with a plan to keep my mom off my back, avoid the doctor, and not get fat.

I decided to take the smallest portions of what my mom served me, and I continued to eat slowly. Whenever possible, I'd skip meals, of course, but if she was around, I'd eat. I knew over time that her vigilance would wane, and then I could go back to eating even less. "Yes!" I congratulated myself. That'd work.

I repeated this cycle with my mom and doctors several times over the next few years until other opportunities to move deeper into "Victimville" came in the form of boys, crushes, and relationships. My body's metabolism caught up with my eating, and I moved into a phase of being able to eat whatever I wanted without gaining weight. This allowed me to turn my full focus on love, love that I wanted, love that I needed—love that would never be mine.

And I would bring this perceived fate to life with the choices I made and the beliefs I held. Though I hated it, railed against it, I believed that it was all I deserved. I believed that I was a perpetual victim—and so I was.

This understanding enlightened my path. This understanding enabled me to make a conscious choice for something different later in my life. I had reached an understanding of what I had created and chosen from that tragic event in my life; an understanding that I had permanently stamped of what I thought was my worth on my body with my tattoo; an understanding that I had cracked open a door into possibilities, a door into a deeper understanding, a door into transformation of the soul.

But first, I needed to understand that being molested may have been the first time I truly felt like a victim; but what had led up to me making the choice to allow it? Because I did allow it. I allowed it by not speaking up.

The time had come for me to tease apart even more of my life; a time for me to dive deeper.

CHAPTER 3
DIVING DEEPER

With the understanding that the way I responded to events came from even further back in my past, I decided to dive deeper into my past and try to figure out where it all began for me.

My mother would tell you that I was a quiet baby—one that she could place on a blanket to play, and there I would remain until she moved me. She would tell you that I had huge eyes and that she loved to dress me up like a little doll. But my first memories are from when I was four years old.

I was inside our little house in San Bernardino, standing on our couch in the living room, peering out the big picture window. I could barely see over the back of that old saggy couch, but I was anxious to watch. My dad had sent me inside because he said it was dangerous out there. I didn't understand what was so dangerous. I had been playing in the yard and hadn't been hurt at all.

I watched him drag a ladder over to the large tree that stood in the middle of our yard. He was dressed funny for such a warm day. He had on warm clothes with long sleeves like he'd wear when it was cold. He wore gloves and a wide-brimmed hat pulled low over his face. I could barely see his sparkling sky-blue eyes, and his normal sweet grin was absent from his handsome face. He carried a large stick in his hand.

With avid curiosity mixed with anxiety, I watched him climb the ladder and begin whacking at the tree, causing the branches to shake and the leaves to drop. A roundish object dropped from the tree and I could see hornets flying all around. They swarmed my dad and the tree.

Inside, safe in our living room, my little body was shaking; tears dripped from my eyes. I was scared for my dad, for I knew hornets stung and hurt. I didn't want my daddy hurt. But that wasn't why I was crying. "Their home. He broke their home," I cried. I felt as though I was a hornet and my home had suddenly been attacked and then disappeared. I was scared, confused, and angry.

My mother's voice cracked into my confused mind, "Stop being silly. He's only taking down the hornets' nest so you won't get hurt."

For me, I only understood that I was feeling several different things at once. Love and fear for my dad, and the hurt and anger of the hornets. How could I be feeling an animal's feelings? It made no sense, as I had never heard anyone else speak of this, and my mom's reaction told me I must be wrong.

The next memory I have, also at the age of four, is feeling another person's feelings. I was at my friend's house across the alley from ours. I liked going over there, as I could go by myself. My mother would watch as I slipped through our gate, crossed the alley, and opened their gate. Today was my friend's birthday party, and I was excited to go.

On this day, as I slipped through their gate, I saw something new in the yard. Hanging from their biggest tree was a piñata, shaped like a horse in bright green, yellow, and blue. The horse was even wearing a funny hat with a wide brim and a round bump on the top. There was a buzz of excitement in the air as people rushed around, greeting the new arrivals and setting up the party.

I quietly walked to where my friend was, slipping unnoticed past the adults. "Hi," she greeted me gaily.

"Happy Birthday!" I whispered, exchanging a happy grin with my friend.

"What is that horse in the tree?" I said as I pointed to it.

"It's a piñata that's got candy and prizes in it for us."

Curious as to how candy and prizes would come out of the funny-looking horse, I sat on a patch of cool grass in the shade of a tall tree. There I could watch the horse and the partygoers at the same time.

As the kids gathered around the piñata, my friend's father explained how it worked. He began calling kids forward to take their turn. One by one he'd blindfold them and put the stick in their hand. He'd spin them in circles and everyone would laugh as they staggered around trying to hit the horse.

I felt the excitement of everyone and clapped along, cheering each person on.

As the piñata broke after a boy gave it a solid whack, I felt the desperation of those around me. "There won't be enough candy. I won't get any." No one was actually saying this, but the words were echoing as loudly in my head as if they'd been shouted in my ear. I became concerned that there wasn't enough for everyone to get some, and I did the only thing I could think to do; I took three pieces of candy and stepped back, letting the other kids continue to grab it up.

As they scooped up handfuls, shrieking with delight, I felt as if I was watching it all from out of my body. I wasn't desperate or concerned about the candy, but I could clearly feel that others were. Again, it was like I was there, but not there. I felt as though other people's feelings dominated my own.

This was when I began to realize that I knew things I shouldn't be able to know. I couldn't explain it. I just knew things about people, animals, and places. Whenever I'd verbalize this aloud, I was met with strange looks. I noticed that people would keep their distance from me.

I can clearly recall a time that a man and his wife visited our home. When I met them, my stomach turned. Something was "bad" about this man. In my mind, I could see as clear as if it was happening in front of me; the man hitting the woman who was his wife, in the face. The image of the man was incongruous with what I knew of him. He appeared peaceful, and was laughing and joking with my parents. I stayed as far away from him as I could.

After they took their leave, I turned to my mom. "Mommy, why does that man hit his wife? Was she bad?"

With a shocked look, Mom replied, "What? He didn't hit her. What are you talking about?"

"Yes he did. Before. He got mad and hit her face."

"I was here the whole time. Nothing like that happened. Quit making stuff up."

"I saw it in my mind, Mommy. It's true."

"That's evil to see things like that. It's the devil's work. You are not to do that anymore. Do you hear me?"

"I can't help what I see in my mind."

"You're doing the devil's work when you talk about it. That's what evil people do. It's a sin."

My mom had called me evil. She said my intuitive abilities were the work of the devil. This confused me, since several psychic phenomena were mentioned in the Bible. Why was it OK back then, but now that it was happening to me, it was evil?

It didn't feel evil. It felt right, strong, and centered. Did that make me evil? My mom said it did—and so I believed it did. I did the best I could over the next several years to ignore those visions, those "knowings," when they appeared to me. I was confused and scared, but I wanted to be good so that I would be loved.

It's hard to be good when every time you turn around you're being told you're wrong or you're bad. It seemed to me that no matter what I did, it was wrong. If I did, by chance, do something right, nothing was said. Silence was my only reward.

As the years passed, the knowledge that I wasn't good enough, smart enough, or just plain enough, grew into a certainty within me. I began to victimize myself.

This was what led to my silence when I was victimized and betrayed by my grandfather. I believed I had done something wrong. I must have. I was always doing something wrong.

When I was little, my mom dressed me in frilly, girly pink dresses. As soon as I was old enough to start choosing for myself, I chose pants and t-shirts. They were more conducive to climbing trees, playing in the dirt, and getting into the occasional scrap that I found myself in.

Often, I would come home with skinned elbows and knees only to hear my mom muttering, "You're supposed to be a girl," under her breath as she cleaned up my scrapes. I found more enjoyment in climbing trees, and playing with spiders, and blue-belly lizards than in being a "proper little girl."

I was often teased about my name, being so short, or being so quiet—anything the bigger, more popular kids could think of, it seemed. I became quite good at tuning them out. I'd bury my nose in a book and get lost in that world. If there were no books available, I'd transport myself into a different world in my head—a world where I was loved, beautiful, and free to do as I wished. I got so good at doing this that one time in class I became so absorbed in a book during reading time that I didn't hear the teacher when he told us to put our books away. I didn't hear the clatter of the other students getting out their necessary papers. I didn't hear the giggles and whispers as the students watched the teacher standing next to me, staring at me, waiting for me to obey.

Suddenly there was a loud slamming sound as if something was trying to hit me and had just missed, hitting the desk next to mine. I jumped upright, sucking in a gasp, prepared to scream and run from the threat.

As the fog in my brain cleared and reality reasserted itself, the sound of laughter reached my ears. Red stole over my face to the tips of my ears as I realized that they were laughing at me because the teacher had dropped a book next to me to get my attention. He snickered, along with the students, as he said, "Welcome back. Now will you put your book away and join the rest of the class in the real world?"

Incidents like this provided more ammunition for the bullies. I never fought back. I would take all those nasty words and feelings and stuff them down into a deep hole inside of my heart. There they would stay until that ugly ol' cynic in my head carted them out to be replayed in all their dark glory, proving how unlovable and unwanted I was.

The only time I had a different reaction was when the bullies picked on someone else. I couldn't stand to see someone else hurting. I didn't want anyone to experience the ache that absorbed my very being. So, when I saw someone else being bullied, I became a different person. A fierce warrior goddess would rise up in me. I'd charge in with no fear, no matter how many bullies were there or how much larger than me they stood.

Once, when I was in the third grade and getting ready to walk home from school with my brother, who was in the fifth grade, we found ourselves surrounded by a half dozen sixth-grade boys.

Startled, I looked at each of the faces of the boys around us. Their expressions ranged from angry to gleeful. As their emotions washed over me, they began to taunt my brother.

"Hey, stupid. Where do you think you're going? Walking your girlfriend home?" They slowly walked around us in a circle, trying to get a rise out of my brother. His face flushed red in contrast to his blond hair. I could feel the nervous energy rolling off him in waves.

"Shut up!" he screeched. "She's my sister."

"Yeah, right. She looks nothing like you. She's your girlfriend. Come on, give her a kiss now."

"Leave us alone. I didn't do anything to you," Bobby said with his hands clenched into fists and shaking.

"Liar!" they shouted back. In the next moment, one of them picked me up and placed me outside the tight circle surrounding my brother, their backs to me.

For some reason, this spurred my warrior into action. I charged at the boy closest to me, hitting him at the knees and causing his body to hit the ground. As he turned over, my small fist connected with his nose and blood spurted out. With a stunned look, he grabbed his nose and scrambled up to run away. I let him go as I was already tackling my next foe.

As the circle of bullies realized they were the ones now being attacked, they scattered. My warrior left three of them with souvenirs; one with a bloody nose, one with a black eye, and one with a fat lip. I felt confident I wouldn't be called into the principal's office for fighting on school grounds, as what sixth-grade boy would confess that a third-grade girl had beaten them up?

Bobby looked at me with something akin to awe and confusion, and then we turned and headed home in silence. We never spoke about that day again, but it remained etched in my memory.

Even throughout all the bullying and minimal friends, I managed to be "boy crazy." In kindergarten I had a boyfriend who was in the third grade. That was the start of a pattern for me, as well. Constantly seeking the love and attention to fill that ache in my heart, I sought older boys. Some part of me believed if they were older maybe they would take care of me, instead of me having to take care of them.

That was how, at the age of thirteen, I found myself "dating" a seventeen-year-old and asking him to teach me how to French kiss. I was tired of hearing how beautiful I would be when I grew up. I wanted to be beautiful now, and thought that if I knew how to kiss like an older girl, I'd be treated like an older girl, and they would call me beautiful now.

John and his friends seemed to like having me around, and he was always very sweet to me. When I asked him to show me how to French kiss, he didn't make fun of me or laugh. Instead he gave me a wicked little grin and asked if I was sure. As I nodded my assent, he pulled me close and leaned down so his deep blue eyes were looking into mine.

My body stilled as my heart raced. I gazed up at him with absolute trust and awaited his instruction, even as I wondered at my own boldness.

He instructed me how wide to open my mouth, showed me how to play with his tongue. He kissed me passionately; he kissed me softly, guiding me each time.

Through it all he graded me. I received C's and then B's and finally A+'s. It was strange and a bit surreal, but I didn't know how else to learn.

What I didn't know was that I was making these choices to please others. My codependency was rapidly developing, disguised as a way to gain love.

CHAPTER 4

I CAN'T EVEN DIE RIGHT

My Sweet Sixteen wasn't all so sweet. I was grounded for my birthday. The man I loved, Ken, had written me from the Army and told me how he was in love with another woman. He was my first true love. He wrote me like I was his younger sister, instead of his soul mate.

I wanted out. Out of this world and this life. I'd had enough. That would show them. They'd all be sorry then. If I was gone they'd realize how much I did for them and how I'd never do anything for them again. After all, wasn't that how it happened in all the romantic movies and novels?

"*No,*" that mean voice whispered. "*They'd probably have a party instead. Celebrate not having to put up with you anymore. You're just crazy and stupid. No one could ever love you.*"

"Ken loved me!" I cried in protest.

"*He left you, didn't he? Just like everyone always does. He found someone better. There'll always be someone better. Do everyone a real favor and just get it over with.*"

With agonizing slowness I dragged myself off the narrow twin bed with its scratchy brown comforter, knocking the odd red and yellow pillows to the ground. It played out like a scene in a bad dramatic movie—though there was no one to watch. *Yes. I should just get it over with*, I agreed with that voice. But one thing first. *Ken has to know how much I truly loved him—even if he doesn't care.*

I stumbled to the window seat and with shaking hands, opened it. Through my teary eyes I found what I was looking for. The box.

The box was an old red shoebox with an "I love Ken" sticker on the lid. The box contained mementos from our relationship. As I took each item from the box, the memories of how we met and how we loved came flooding in.

It was my first day of high school. I had ridden the bus and spent the whole time in nervous anticipation of what high school would bring for me. So far no one had even talked to me, and I was beginning to wonder if the next four years would bring me more of the same.

When the bus finally came to a stop, I rose on shaking legs and did my best to blend in with the other students as we filed off the bus. As I stepped off the last step, I looked up and saw my older brother, Bob, standing there with two other guys.

Crap! Here it comes. The teasing is going to start before I even get to see what the campus looks like. Instead of the teasing, I heard a low whistle.

"Wow! Is that your sister? How come you never told me you had a gorgeous sister?" came from one of the guys standing with my brother. He was around five foot nine with dark hair, brown eyes, and a mustache. He had socked Bob in the arm and was gazing at me with a smile. I found him cute and was pleased that he appeared to mean what he had said.

His name was Rod. Silently standing with Rod and Bob was Ken. As I was introduced, my breath caught in my throat. With smoky green eyes, Ken smiled a crooked smile down at me from his six foot one lanky frame. His black hair framed his handsome face. Wow! If only he would think I was worth looking at.

Over the next few weeks, I found myself hanging out more and more with Rod and Ken, even though I was only a freshman and they were juniors. Rod and I even dated briefly, but Ken always captured my attention and made my heart beat.

One day, as we were sitting around watching a movie, I felt fingers brush the side of my leg. Glancing down to be sure I wasn't imagining it, I saw Ken's fingers moving slowly along my thigh. I looked up and met his smoky green eyes with my hazel ones. My heart sped up when he leaned over and whispered in my ear, "Can I kiss you?"

I could only nod in awe as words escaped me. As he leaned in and lightly brushed his lips against mine, my body felt as though it melted into a puddle. All our other friends, including Rod, my ex-boyfriend, who were in the room completely faded away, forgotten. There was only Ken.

Moments later, the sound of catcalls, laughter, and whistles made their way into my consciousness. Feeling the heat of my blush, I met Ken's eyes once more to see if he, too, was laughing. Was it all a joke?

Ken wrapped his large comforting hand around mine and gave it a squeeze. "Shut up!" he said to the others. "She's mine now."

"His!" my heart sang. Yes. At last I would have the love I dreamed of but never thought possible. Ken was always kind, polite, and humorous. I thought he was the best looking guy I had ever seen. I fell instantly, deeply and completely in love.

We were inseparable for the next year. I secretly dreamed and planned our life together. I was convinced that at last someone loved me as much as I loved him. I saved every memento I could from our dates together. A small vase with the dried rose and baby's breath, ticket stubs, notes, stickers that said, "I love Ken." a shoestring with hearts, and other little things. Then the first heartbreak with Ken happened.

I overheard a girl at school telling her friends that she was now going out with Ken. My Ken. I was devastated. Barely registering her snide grin that she tossed my way, I went to confront Ken, hoping that it was just a vicious lie and that I was hurt over nothing.

When I finally found him it was like someone else was in his body. He didn't act like my Ken. He stood stiffly and his eyes wouldn't meet mine.

"What the hell is going on, Ken?"

"What do you mean?"

"I overheard some bitch say she was dating you now."

"Yeah, so?"

"What? What about us?" His only response to this question was a shoulder shrug.

"Were you even going to tell me? What did I do wrong?" I fired the questions at him, feeling desperate now.

"I'm just moving on."

I was confused, hurt, and scrambling to figure out what I had done to cause him to leave me. As I struggled with what I could say to make him love me again, he turned and walked away.

Over the next several weeks, I pulled away from everyone. I numbly did my schoolwork and just existed. I certainly didn't feel alive. I just felt like a worthless blob. I barely paid attention to everyone around. So little, in fact, that it took some time for me to realize that Ken was gone. He had moved out of state.

He had to move clean out of state to get away from me. What could I have possibly done to make him hate me so? Months later I got my answer—though it was not what I expected.

I was walking down the street with my friend, Michele. Suddenly, in the middle of my sentence, I froze. Not only had my mouth stopped moving, but my body as well. Michele had continued on for a few more paces and then realized I was no longer by her side. She stopped and turned around, looking at me questionably.

"Ken's back," I said, looking at her with shock.

"What? Did you see his car drive by?"

"No. I just know. He's back."

"Oh-kaayyyy." Michele knew I had intuitive hits from time to time, but this seemed incredible.

"I have to go home. He's going to call," I said as I turned and began sprinting toward my house.

"Call me later," she yelled to my retreating back.

Within five minutes of my bursting into our house, the phone rang. "I've got it." I yelled, making a mad dash for the phone.

"Hello?" I said breathlessly into the phone.

"Hello, beautiful. I'm home and want to see you."

It was Ken. He was back and wanting to see me. He hadn't left me forever after all.

"Come see me now," I happily demanded.

"On my way."

As I hung up the phone, I felt something I hadn't felt for months—a smile on my face.

Ken came over and we went for a walk through the neighborhood so we could talk without anyone listening. He told me the reason he broke up with me the way he did was because he knew he was moving. He didn't want me to hang on and wait for him. He didn't know then if he would ever be back and didn't want my life to be spent waiting for him. He said he didn't know any other way to do it. He also said the reason he was home now was because his father, whom he had been living with, had killed himself. My heart hurt for his pain, his loss, and yet was filled with joy that he was back, and with me. I forgave him instantly. More mementos went into that little red shoebox over the next few months.

Soon, Ken graduated from high school and entered the Army, once again leaving me behind. This time was different, though. We talked it through. We would not be together as a couple, though we would still write. We would be free to date other people, though I professed my undying love, and would see what happened when he was finished serving. I was still sad to see him go, but not devastated. He was my first true love, and I just knew in my heart that we would find our way back to each other again.

Instead, I held a crumbled letter in my hand. His scrawled handwriting told me that my dream was dead. He would not be coming back for me. He was with her. For an instant I felt a seething hatred toward the woman, even though she was completely unknown to me. She had ripped my heart to shreds. She had stolen my Pooky Bear, my Ken.

Quickly, the pain dissolved the anger and turned it inward. *Of course he found someone better, you stupid twit. Why on earth would he want you?* Thrusting his now crumbled letter into the red box, I pulled out his picture and placed it where I could look at it as I began to write my own letter.

My Dearest Pooky Bear,

I received your letter today, telling me you found someone new. I hope she makes you happy. I wish it could've been me that made you feel happy. I wish I were so smart and pretty that you couldn't wait to get back here to me. But we both know that isn't so.

You were my heart, my whole world. I wanted nothing more than to spend my life doing whatever I could to make you happy. This world is just not worth living in without you.

I wanted to write you this letter to make sure that you don't blame yourself. I want you to be happy. I know, deep in my soul, that you are the only one for me. If I cannot be with you, I will love you from heaven. You will be happier that way.

Please remember me fondly. I wanted you to have this box of little things I saved throughout our time together, so you can remember me now and then. I will love you forever.

Love, Giggles

As the tears streamed down my face, I folded up the letter and placed it at the top of the box. I closed the lid and wrote on the top of the box, "This box is confidential. It is to be given to Kenneth upon my death."

With a sigh I placed the box on the window seat where it could be easily found. I wiped at my tears and took a few deep breaths. OK. That's done. Now—how should I do it? I climbed back onto my bed, hugging a red pillow as I contemplated which would be the best way to take my life.

I could use my dad's gun. I pictured my mother finding me in the bathroom with my brains splattered on the walls. I could see her pushing open the door after I didn't respond to her yelling at me to get out of the bathroom. I could see the color drain from her face as she took in the red, chunky splatter with gray matter on the beige walls. No, no. I couldn't do that to her. I didn't want her to find me that way. I didn't want a bloody mess left for her to clean up.

I could take pills, overdose. I envisioned myself swallowing the pills and just peacefully drifting away. Hmmmmm—I didn't have any prescriptions, but I bet I could find something. I wondered how many I would need to take. OK. That was a possibility.

I could slit my wrists. I pictured myself sitting in the bath, cutting my wrists and watching as my crimson-colored blood mixed with the water. I would only feel a momentary pain, and then I would drift in unconsciousness as my body bled out. Another possibility.

While trying to decide which way to kill myself, and exhausted from crying, I drifted off to sleep, envisioning my funeral. They'd cry, because that's what you're supposed to do when someone you know dies. They'd talk about how tragic it was. And then they'd move on. They'd be happier, even relieved at no longer having to deal with me. I would quickly become just a faint memory.

As I sluggishly walked to my bus stop the next morning, I received inspiration for another way to die a quick death. A large semi-truck had sped past me, blowing my hair back. I turned to watch it as it sped by, the wheels almost as tall as I was. *Wow! If that were to run me over, I'm sure I wouldn't survive.*

Morosely cheered a little at the thought, I couldn't wait to get through school so I could walk home and find another semi to do the deed.

As it turned out, I would have to wait a few more weeks for another semi-truck to come my way. As we didn't live off of a main road, they rarely drove in the areas I regularly walked.

Then one day it happened. I heard the low rumble of a big semi-truck in the distance. I scanned the road ahead of me, praying it was coming my way. There! A flash of a chrome grill in the sunlight up ahead. This is it!

As the truck neared I could see the big blue cab with the large grill that grew larger as it drew nearer. It looked like a large monster, bearing down. I slowed my walk, trying to anticipate the best time to step in front of the truck without giving him time to swerve. *That monster can have me for dinner.* I took a step over the white line separating the cars from bikes and pedestrians.

As I lifted my other foot to take what I hoped would be my last step, I looked up. My eyes locked onto the terrified truck driver. His mouth was open in a big O. He looked as though he was rising off his seat as his hands gripped the wheel with his arms locked at the elbows. Without thought, I stepped back into the safety of that beat-up white line. The truck sped by with just a slight swerve, a delayed reaction to my step outside the white line.

I couldn't do it. I couldn't leave someone to blame themselves for my death. When the first truck had breezed by me, all I saw then was the truck, the machine, and a quick way out. When my eyes had locked with the driver of this truck, the reality of what that could do to the driver had come crashing in. This was not the way for me to check out.

Feeling the weight of uselessness like an elephant sitting on my chest and shoulders, I slowly finished the walk home. *Alright. The truck thing won't work, so I'll do it in the bath tonight,* I told myself as I trudged the last few feet to my house.

As I let myself in, I noticed that my mother was upstairs. *The perfect opportunity to smuggle a knife from the kitchen in preparation for tonight.* I scurried into the kitchen and grabbed a steak knife from the drawer, hiding it in my backpack.

I spent the next few hours trying to distract myself so time would fly by and bath time would arrive.

That evening as I prepared for what I prayed was my final bath, I felt very somber and yet filled with an odd anticipation of relief. The mirror in our little bathroom was fogged with the steam from my bath. *Good. Now I don't have to see my ugly face again,* I said to myself as I quickly stripped off my clothes. I looked around the beige bathroom accented with blue towels and rugs, and then I grabbed my clothes and balled them up tight, throwing them into the old mustard-colored hamper. My fingers closed around the black handle of the knife, gripping it tight as I lifted it off the bathroom counter.

As I stepped into the hot water, I was careful to point the blade down and away from me in case I slipped. I laughed when I realized what I was doing. Practicing knife safety as if it mattered if I slipped and stabbed myself. I mean, I was planning to kill myself after all, and it seemed a bit ridiculous.

I eased my body into the water, hot little waves lapping at my skin. I sat with my legs straight out in front of me and laid my arm across my leg, turning my wrist up. I took the knife and ran it lightly down my wrist, mimicking the action that I would take with pressure. Lengthwise cut, not across. I had studied suicide attempts and knew the quickest and most reliable way was lengthwise down the wrist.

I sat still as a statue with the blade pressed against my wrist. *Come on, you chicken-shit! Do it. Get on with it!* I egged myself on in my tortured head. Yet I couldn't seem to move. I couldn't apply the pressure. I couldn't do it. After an hour, the water had cooled and my skin was chilled. I finally moved.

Numb with disappointment, I set the knife on the floor beside the tub. I sat and watched the water drain away, slicking off my skin and down the drain in a swirl. *See? You don't even have the guts to do everyone a favor and off yourself,* the critic within snarled.

I sighed and slowly climbed from the tub. After drying myself off and dressing for bed, I hid the knife in the bathroom cupboard, hiding the evidence of what I had tried to do.

I climbed into bed, seeing only one option left—overdose. Tomorrow I would search the medicine cabinets and see what I could find. Weary from my inner battle, I quickly fell into a dreamless sleep.

In the downstairs cabinet, the next day, I found a packet of Sudafed. It was the only pill I could find with enough of a supply that was supposedly lethal if you took too much. I hid it in my pants and made my way upstairs to stash it away until it was time for bed. I figured I could take them all just before bed and then I would go to sleep and peacefully drift away.

That evening I stood in front of the mirror in our little beige bathroom and watched with fascination as I swallowed each pill in the packet one by one. *This is finally it.* I congratulated myself as the last pills in the pack disappeared down my throat.

Struck by a sudden urge to say goodbye to my mother, I went down the stairs and stood in the darkly paneled living room with its faded furniture, waiting for her to come out of the laundry room.

"What are you doing down here?" she asked with a slight start at seeing me just standing there, when I was supposed to be in bed.

"Just came to say goodnight."

"Are you OK? You look pale."

I shrugged my shoulders and said, "I'm fine, just tired. Goodnight."

I could feel her eyes boring into my back as I slowly made my way back up the stairs, thinking, *that will be the last time I see her.*

As I lay on my bed, stretched out on my back, I felt very heavy, as though there were rocks instead of bones in my body. My breathing was shallow, and my eyelids were too heavy to lift for one last look around.

Goodbye, world. I don't know why I was even born, but I won't be anyone's problem now, was my last conscious thought.

The next morning, the sun peeped through my window shades and fell across my face. I awoke with a jolt. I was still alive. *Damn! I can't even die right,* was the first thought to run through my head, followed closely by, *Now what?*

Figuring I was stuck living because I was so screwed up that I couldn't even kill myself properly, I thought I might as well see if I could find some way to be somewhat happy. I knew I didn't deserve true love, but I still had a small kernel of desperate hope that someone would love me a little.

That would have to be good enough, because I sure wasn't going to get more.

With a resigned heart, I put away Ken's little red box and began to try to find a way to cope with living again.

CHAPTER 5

BABIES HAVING BABIES

Since it looked like I was doomed to live, and true love was no longer possible for me.—I didn't deserve it anyway—I stopped saving myself. I had held onto my virginity like a closely guarded present, waiting to give it to my love in marriage. I hadn't even slept with Ken yet, planning to give myself to him on our wedding night that I'd so carefully planned and dreamed about.

Being a virgin no longer mattered to me. It now just seemed like another burden, another reason for guys to steer clear of me. I knew about sex. I knew how it worked, but I didn't know much else.

All I had been told by my mother, besides the basic facts of how it worked, was that you don't do it until you're married. Period. No discussion of birth control. It wasn't an option in our house. I knew about the pill and condoms from the sex ed. classes in school, but I had no idea how to go about getting them without my parents finding out.

Consequences of pregnancy or STDs seemed very remote compared to the consequence of my mom finding birth control in my possession, even if I could get my hands on it. I didn't say I was logical; this was just my thought process at the time.

Not being in love with anybody at the time, I had made this decision. I wanted my first time to be with someone I knew and could trust to treat me well without wanting a relationship. I chose Rod, the mutual friend of Ken's and mine. We had briefly dated before Ken and I got together. Rod knew me. He knew I would always love Ken. He also treated me well, and we had remained good friends.

Rod's birthday had just passed and I hadn't gotten him a gift yet. I thought this was very serendipitous. I would give him my virginity as his birthday gift. That night I wrote him a note to be delivered the next day.

Happy Belated Birthday, Rod—My Teddy Bear!

I have a surprise for you for your birthday! Please come over to my house tomorrow afternoon at 1:00 to get your birthday gift!

Love,
Becca

Rod arrived the next day promptly at 1:00. No one else was home.

"What's my surprise?" he asked, dancing around like a little kid.

"Guess!" I said with a wicked grin, knowing he would never guess. When we were dating I had made it clear that I wasn't ready to go all the way and that I was saving myself.

"Ummmm—a teddy bear," he said with a grin, obviously enjoying the game. I shook my head.

"A new car."

"Nope! You'll never guess."

"A kiss."

"You're close."

"Really? Wow! Now I really want to know. What is it?" he said with surprised anticipation.

I leaned close, with my cheeks flaming, and whispered, "Me."

His face, a mixture of excitement and curiosity at what I could possibly mean by that simple statement, stared back at mine. "What exactly do you mean by that? You want to get back together?"

"No. I want you to make love to me. Be my first."

"Are you sure? No relationship, just this?"

"Absolutely. Happy Birthday," I said, feigning confidence.

I took him by the hand and led him up to my room. Fifteen minutes later, after much fumbling hands and heavy breathing, mingled with a few wet kisses, the deed was done.

"Are you alright? I didn't hurt you, did I?" Rod asked with concern as I lay there, naked and trying to mask my thoughts.

"You didn't hurt me. You were wonderful." I smiled at him, while in my mind I was thinking, *is that all there is to it? What's the big deal?* If all sex was like that I wasn't sure what all the hype was about. It's not that he was bad; it just didn't affect me the way I thought it would. It all seemed rather droll to me.

"This was the best birthday present ever. Thank you," Rod said as he gave me one last kiss and began to dress. I rolled off the bed and pulled my clothes on as well so I could see him to the door.

After this I began to flirt more with a variety of men, resulting in lots of dates. Rod and I remained friends but didn't date again. I didn't know what I was searching for other than the temporary attention that made me feel good. I was having fun setting my sights on a guy and then flirting until I snagged him.

It was one of these guys that took me to my homecoming dance that year. His name was Brian, and he was tall and slender with blonde hair and blue eyes. He was good looking and very sweet. Best of all was that he lived four hours away. I thought this would ensure that it would stay lighthearted. I had told him about the upcoming dance, and he offered to take me. I accepted, thinking it would be fun to bring someone from outside the school.

Between the time I accepted and the time of the dance, Ken came back to town. Again, I was one of his first phone calls. How easily the sound of his voice pulled me back in. How quickly those feelings rose to the surface, as if they had been lying in wait for him. I struggled to not be so accessible, to not let him know how he affected me.

"I'm back, my sweet Giggles. I missed you."

"Welcome back."

"What? I'm not your Pooky Bear anymore?"

"You'll always be my Pooky Bear. I just didn't want to upset your girl-friend. Did she come back with you?"

"There is no girlfriend."

"Oh." I didn't know what to say to this, as my heart had leapt into my throat knowing he was free. Yet my mind was screaming, *No! Not again. He'll only be around till someone better comes along.*

"I know you have homecoming coming up next week."

"Yeah." Now was my opportunity to show him that he wasn't the only one who could find someone else. "I'm going with this guy I met. He lives in Danville, but he's coming all the way here just to take me."

"Tell him you can't go with him. I'm taking you."

I was stunned. I was elated. I was heartbroken. All within a space of seconds.

"I can't do that. It wouldn't be fair to him."

"So what? Just tell him you can't go. Make something up."

"No. I won't do that. He's sweet and I already committed to going with him."

"I'm going to get you to change your mind, you know."

"I don't think so. I always keep my word, and you know that." I retorted, secretly pleased that he was fighting to take me.

I wouldn't give in and do that to Brian. It wouldn't be fair, but a part of me wanted to do exactly what Ken said, to call Brian and tell him not to come—no matter that he had already ordered a tux and my flowers. No matter that we had already arranged for him to spend the night at my house in a separate room, of course, because he lived so far away. No matter that he had done nothing to warrant it.

Though it hurt me to turn Ken down, in my heart I knew I had to do the right thing and keep my date with Brian.

The time for the dance arrived, and Brian was as sweet in person as he had been on the phone. The difference was that my thoughts now strayed constantly to Ken. I wasn't fully present for the entire dance. Brian looked very handsome in his tux. He brought me a beautiful corsage. He remained respectful, devoted, and attentive to me throughout the evening. He didn't seem to notice anything was amiss.

When the dance was over and Brian had taken me home, he gave me a goodnight kiss before going inside. I'm sure he meant it to be passionate, but I felt like I was kissing a fish. It was wet. His mouth opened and closed over mine, but no tongue was involved. All the attraction was gone for me. My heart was back with Ken, wondering how different the evening would've been if I had gone with him. Brian didn't even seem to notice my lack of enthusiasm as I kissed him back.

The next day after Brian had returned to Danville, a dozen red roses arrived. Once I discovered they were from Brian and not Ken, I only felt disappointment as I looked at them. My mother was more enthused about the roses than I was.

"Wow! A dozen red roses. How nice is that?" she exclaimed.

"Yeah, they're nice." I said with a shrug.

"What's the matter with you? It's the first time any guy has ever sent you a dozen roses, and you act like you don't care."

"I don't like him that much."

"You're such an ingrate. You don't deserve a guy to treat you so nice."

That's true, I thought to myself. I was being ungrateful, but I couldn't help the way I felt. To my mom I just gave her my normal, tuned out, blank look.

With a heavy sigh she arranged the roses on the hall table, demanded I write him a thank you note, and left me standing there wondering why I couldn't like someone like Brian instead of Ken.

Later that evening, when Ken called and asked me out for the following weekend, I readily accepted, knowing I couldn't deny my love for him.

When his battered orange pinto pulled up to the house for our date, I couldn't stop the shivers of delight racing down my spine. At long last, I was going to make love to Ken, my one true love. He didn't know, yet, that I was no longer that virginal little girl. I couldn't wait to see the delighted shock on his face when I told him. We were going to the drive-in to see a movie. It didn't matter to me which one, as I had no intention of seeing it. I planned to keep him busy the whole time. I thought that since I would have sex now, he would have no reason to look elsewhere.

"Hello, beautiful!" Ken greeted me with his sexy, crooked smile when I opened the door to his knock.

"Hey there, yourself. Let's get going." I replied with enthusiasm.

"Wait. I've got to say hi to your mom first." Ken was very well mannered, something that earned him big points with my parents.

With a reluctant sigh, I stepped aside so he could come in, and I led him to my mom in the kitchen. After they exchanged greetings and Ken let her know when he would have me home, we finally left. By this time, I felt like I was jumping out of my skin. I wanted to kiss him so badly.

As I settled into the Pinto's bucket seat, I felt his eyes on my skin. I lifted my eyes to meet his in anticipation. The rest of the world disappeared from my awareness as his soft lips drew close.

With passion born from love and restrained by tenderness, usually reserved for lovers, his lips closed on mine while our tongues danced a wild tango. When we came up for air, energy sparked and crackled between us. This, yes this, was what I wanted forever.

With a mischievous glint in his sexy green eyes, he gave me a wink and started the car, heading for the drive-in. As if the kiss wasn't enough to have me fall in love with him all over again, he began to tell me what he did the night of the homecoming dance.

"So how was your date with that guy?"
"It was OK."
"Just OK, huh?"
"Yeah. Why?" I wondered why he was asking about my date with someone else. Was he worried that I liked Brian? Was he jealous?
"I came looking for you that night."
"You did not." I said in disbelief. "You didn't come to the dance."
"I did, too!"
"How'd you get in? You're not a student there anymore."
"They let me in because I'm an alumni."
"How come I didn't see you, then?"
"I searched that whole dance floor for you."
"What would you have done if you'd found me?"
"I would've taken you out of there," he said with a defiant grin.
In disbelief, I said, "No way! You're making that up."
"No, I'm not. Ask around. I was looking for you."
"Why?" I asked with curiosity.
"Because you should have been there with me, not him."

As we pulled into the drive-in, my mind spun out the fantasy of how different homecoming could've been if Ken had indeed found me. I could see him coming into the dance and pulling me out of Brian's arms, saying, "She's mine! Back off!" and then lifting me into his strong arms and carrying me away. He would've told me he loved me still, and this time we'd be together forever.

My heart filled even more full with love for Ken as my imagined scenario gave me everything I wished for.

Forgotten was the betrayal and hurt each time he left me. He was my first love. My only love. I decided on the spot that I would name my firstborn after him.

We picked our spot to park, as far away from everyone else as we could get. Ken spread a blanket in the back and we clamored over the seats to stretch out and view the movie through the back hatch of that old orange pinto.

By the time the movie was over, Ken had to use a squeegee on the inside of the windshield because we had fogged up the windows so much. Now I thought I knew what all the fuss was about sex. What a difference there was between making love and just doing it. I was in euphoria and never wanted to leave it.

My worst fears and anxieties were realized when Ken once again began to drift away from me just weeks later. Angry and hurt, but only allowing myself to feel the anger, I lashed out by flirting with and dating every guy I could. I wouldn't sleep with anyone, but I sure made them think I would. At least that was true until Doug entered the picture.

One day, as my friend Marla and I were in Old Sacramento just hanging out at a Wendy's and flirting with guys, I saw someone who captured my full attention. He could have been Ken's twin. His body was different. Where Ken was tall and lanky, he was short and stocky. But his face was that same handsome, sexy face with that wicked little grin. I immediately set my cap for him.

I made eye contact with him and sent an "I want you" vibe through the air. We flirted with our eyes while Marla and I chatted. Fortunately, he was with a friend too, as two possible hookups always made it easier.

Noticing that they were making moves to leave, Marla and I left first, ensuring that we passed by them. As we did, I gave a wink with a smile and quirked my head, indicating he should follow me out, all done in one smooth, flowing motion, so to anyone not directly in my line of sight, it didn't appear I'd done anything other than move my head.

A few feet down the wooden walkway, I heard a deep voice say, "Hey! Wait up." I flashed a grin at Marla and turned to see Ken's twin and his friend walking toward us. As we flirted and exchanged numbers, a fantasy ran through my head.

Maybe I wasn't supposed to be with Ken after all. Maybe I was supposed to be with this guy, Doug. Maybe being with Ken was just getting me ready for Doug. They looked so much alike that it was easy to let my feelings for Ken transfer to Doug. I could see us falling in love and marrying right after I graduated from high school. He was twenty-one and I was almost seventeen; surely he could wait a couple of years.

We made plans for a date as Marla and Doug's friend did the same. When the time came for our date, I had myself thoroughly convinced that Doug and I were at the start of being together forever. I was wholly immersed in my fantasy world, so much so that I slept with him on that first date.

Immediately after the deed was done, an intuitive bit of reality slipped in. In that moment, the thought "I'm pregnant" screamed in my head as bold as you please. Quickly dismissing it as impossible—after all, we had only just done it—I slipped back into my comfortable fantasy world.

Six weeks later, I realized that momentary bit of intuitive reality was accurate. I did indeed get pregnant that night. The blue line on the pregnancy test stick proved it. I was scared out of my mind. My parents would kill me! Doug no longer called me. What would he do? I couldn't raise a baby by myself. I was only about to turn seventeen. How would I support it? I was in a panic.

In my panic, I called the hospital to schedule an abortion. My heart squeezed tightly, aching for that little innocent soul, yet believing I had to do this. Assuring me of their confidentiality policy, they scheduled me in two weeks. A sigh of relief that they wouldn't tell my parents escaped me, followed by a sharp pain in my heart thinking of what would happen to my baby. Try as I might, I couldn't convince myself it was anything other than an innocent soul, slowly growing into a human form.

I cried every day for the next week, my arm curled protectively around my slightly rounded stomach. The closer the day came, the more I didn't want to do it. The more I couldn't do it. I knew that whatever choice I made, abortion, adoption, or keeping the baby, I would have to live with that decision the rest of my life. What could I live with?

The first day of my senior year in high school came, and I went, pretending to be normal. Inside, I was still trying to decide what to do. In the middle of third period, my mother showed up and yanked me out of class. She was furious. I began to shake all over as she led me to the parking lot by my arm.

"I know you're pregnant!" she yelled through clenched teeth. "You are not getting an abortion, you little slut. I cannot believe you were so stupid."

Stunned that she knew about the abortion, I snapped back, "How did you find out? That's supposed to be confidential."

"They called me. You're under eighteen."

"They told me that didn't matter. They weren't supposed to call you."

"Well, they did, and now I know. You won't be getting an abortion, and if you try to give it up for adoption, I'll adopt it."

"I had already decided to cancel the abortion anyway," I retorted. "I can't go through with it. But if I decide on adoption, you will not be the one adopting my child."

"Do you even know who the father is?" she said in disgust.

The question knocked the wind from my anger. Did she really think so low of me? Feeling like the cheap whore she thought I was, I stated, "Yes, I do. But he doesn't know yet."

"You're going to tell him. You're going to the doctor for a proper checkup and then we're going to figure out what to do with you," she said and then turned her back on me and strode off to her car.

"Well, this is going to be a stellar year," I said sarcastically as I dropped, weary with the knowledge that my life had now spun once more out of control, onto the curb to contemplate how I would get through the day, the week, the year—heck! How would I make it through my life?

By the time my doctor's visit arrived, I had made up my mind about what I would do with my baby. I examined each choice carefully and chose what I knew I could live with the best. I knew it wasn't going to be easy, no matter what I chose. I could understand abortion, especially in cases of rape. But that didn't apply here, and it would've been a choice that haunted me forever. I could understand adoption. I knew it was an unselfish act in many ways. I also knew that I would always worry and wonder if my baby was being loved and taken care of properly. I loved children. I had a natural affinity for them. They were as drawn to me as I was to them. I had even worked at a daycare center for a year, and it just made me love them more. For me, the only option was to keep my baby.

I called Doug to let him know. The conversation was not what I hoped for, but it was what I expected.

"Congratulations! You're a daddy." I led off the conversation, figuring I might as well get to the point.

"What? How do you know it's mine?" he exclaimed in anger.

"I know. There was no one else."

"Well, then you're getting an abortion, right?"

"No."

"Then you have to give it up for adoption," he said with the edge of desperation beginning to creep into his voice.

"I don't have to do any such thing. I'm keeping it."

There was an audible click as he hung up. No other questions. No reassurance. Just a buzzing in my ear as the dial tone replaced the momentary silence after that loud click.

I tried several times over the next few months to get in contact with Doug. The only response I got was his mother telling me he had moved out of state. I never heard from him again.

At the doctor's office, they confirmed I was pregnant and told me everything was fine. At the end of the appointment, the doctor sat me in his office and proceeded to voice his opinion on my pregnancy.

"You're ruining your life by having this baby. You have other options," he stated as if he was talking to an idiot.

"I am not ruining my life. I know it will be difficult, but not ruined."

"I think you were forced into keeping this baby. I don't think you know what you're doing."

What was he doing? Trying to get me to have an abortion? I had never experienced a doctor talking to a patient this way. I was confused and angry. What did he think I was, a mindless idiot?

"You obviously don't know me very well if you think anyone can make my mind up for me. I made this decision."

"You're a baby having a baby. You have no idea what a mistake you're making." he stated with a reddening face. I could tell he was getting angry at not being able to sway my mind. It just made me dig my heels in further.

"I think I did make a mistake in coming to you!" I said as I stood and turned to leave. Though nothing more was said, I could feel the daggers stabbing my back as I exited his office.

What that doctor didn't tell me that day caused me a considerable amount of pain and devastation later. I didn't know I was carrying twins. I didn't know I was supposed to stay off my feet, as the placenta had not attached in my uterus. Instead, I was working eight hours a day on my feet. Perhaps he thought I would miscarry and then things in his eyes would be right.

A month later, while at work, I began to experience cramping. Those cramps were worse than any I had ever experienced. The pain stole through my sides, taking my breath away. I doubled over, holding my stomach, but no change of position seemed to help. Frightened, I made my way to the bathroom. I thought I had felt something leak from my body.

When I got into the stall and sat down, I took a few deep breaths, trying to ease the cramping. They seemed to come in waves. I was getting very scared now, as I could feel moisture in my underwear. When I finally managed to look, I saw thick blood that looked very different from period blood. Now I knew for sure something was horribly wrong.

I cleaned myself up as best I could and made my way to the doctor. On the way there, I experienced conflicting feelings. I was scared that I had lost the baby. I felt a hint of relief if I had. I felt instant guilt over that hint of relief. I was sorry for the little soul if it was lost.

At the doctor's office, the truth was revealed. I had switched doctors, and this was the first time I was seeing this one. She listened for the baby's heartbeat and declared it good. This eased my worry until she looked at my chart and then stated, "OK. First let's see if the placenta has reattached itself."

"What?" I said, blinking in disbelief.

"Weren't you told about this?" she asked, her brows knitting together in confusion. "You were supposed to stay off your feet until it had reattached."

"No. No one told me. I've been working eight-hour shifts on my feet this whole time," I said through gritted teeth. Anger at that self-righteous doctor had me seeing red. How dare he try to make that decision for me.

"Well, that certainly explains the reason for the cramping and bleeding," she said.

After a thorough exam, she determined that I had been pregnant with twins and had miscarried one of the babies. It was unusual to only lose one. Knowing that affirmed my belief that I had made the right decision in keeping this baby. He or she was meant to be here. I blamed that first doctor for the loss of the second baby.

Other than being a pregnant teen who was continuously pointed at and whispered about, the rest of the pregnancy was uneventful. I had a healthy little boy. I kept my promise that I'd made to myself; I named him after my first love. I named him Benjamin Kenneth. Benjamin meant "favorite son," and I took one look at him and knew he would be so. Kenneth, well, that was for Ken. He may not have been his, but he sure looked like him. If Ken couldn't love me forever, then Benjamin Kenneth would—as his mom.

I completed my senior year of high school at a young parents program and was able to graduate with my class at my regular high school. I was the only one there with a three-month-old baby, but hey! At least I finished my schooling. I got to walk the diploma walk with the one friend who hadn't abandoned me during my pregnancy—Marla.

Marla and I continued our friendship and continued to "man hunt" together, too. Even though I had a baby, it didn't stop me from dating. If anything, it increased my desire to find my Mr. Right.

I dated pretty much anyone who asked, as long as they were older boys and had no problem with my parenthood. I had no problem getting dates. It was keeping a relationship going that proved elusive.

CHAPTER 6

THIS IS WHAT I DESERVE

The dating frenzy was easy to fall into. I dated a different guy practically every week. It became a joke among my friends and me, trying to keep all their names straight. In my mind I was looking for my Mr. Right. In reality I was done with a guy as soon as he began to be attached. No one lasted more than a couple of weeks.

Time had lost all meaning for me. If you were to ask me, though, each relationship lasted much longer. Any hint of a solid connection and I fell in love. For days that man was the center of my world. With the exception of my son, no one else existed. The same fantasy would spin out in my mind over and over, just with a different face each time in the dream.

This was the one. He would fall helplessly in love with my son and me. He would propose on one knee. He would adopt my son. We would live happily ever after.

I was so caught up in the whirlwind, I never noticed that the guy wasn't there with me. I was too busy becoming the person I thought he wanted. I knew I wasn't really good enough for anyone, so I thought that if I worked real hard at it, I could be the person they said they liked.

This guy liked preppy-type girls, so I wore collared shirts tucked in and Vans tennis shoes. That guy liked rocker girls, so I wore half shirts with the sleeves cut off and bandanas. I observed and changed, trying to conform to their perceived needs. I met guys everywhere I went. It seemed all I had to do was put out the "I'm available" vibe and there they were. One would think that with all that attention, my self-confidence would be boosted. It wasn't. One thing I learned was that if you don't know who you are and what your values and boundaries are, it's almost impossible to believe in yourself.

One of our favorite hangouts was The Mineshaft, a miniature golf course by day and a dance club for sixteen and older at night. There was no alcohol served, but being only eighteen, we didn't care. It was a place to dance and meet guys. One night, while dancing at The Mineshaft with my friends, I met a real cutie named Matt.

Matt was about five foot eleven, with broad shoulders, a trim waist, and gorgeous, big brown eyes. He had dark hair and a killer smile. He was twenty-three and just my type; I liked them older. I thought if the guy was older, the chances were greater of getting my romantic fantasy fulfilled. He also didn't seem to mind that I had a kid. That was always one of my first "tests" with a new guy. I used it as a process of elimination. If I mentioned my son and he made excuses to get away from me, I knew he wasn't worth my time.

Matt was there with his friend and roommate, Frank. While none of my friends seemed interested in Frank, it made it easier to chat as a group. Frank was around the same height as Matt with a little thicker build. He had blue eyes and closely-cut brown hair. He was good looking, too, but I just didn't find him as attractive as Matt. He seemed nice enough, but something gave me a flat feeling when I focused on him.

Most of the dates Matt and I went on, Frank tagged along. It was kind of like I was dating both of them at the same time. We went to the lake; Frank came along. We went to the movies; Frank came along. Matt cooked me a dinner at his house; Frank was there. So it seemed kind of natural to accept when Frank asked me out to dinner. Matt and I had gotten to the point where we fell into the "just friends" category, so it wasn't like I was cheating on him.

Since the date appeared to be casual, I agreed to meet Frank at his and Matt's house before we went to dinner. I had been to their house a few times and felt comfortable there, but for some reason on this night I felt nervous as I knocked on the door.

Frank answered the door with a smile. "Come on in." He said, standing back, yet close enough that I had to brush up against him to come in the door. He was wearing tight jeans and a collared shirt and wore some cologne that smelled like spice and the outdoors with pine and sandalwood.

I slipped past Frank and headed to the living room, looking for Matt. Matt was comfortable. Matt made me feel secure. I adored him, even though I knew we were better off as friends than as lovers. I met an empty room and turned to find Frank watching me.

"Where's Matt?" I asked, "I wanted to say hi before we go to dinner."

"He's off on some date," Frank replied, watching to see my reaction.

"Oh. No problem. So what's the plan for us tonight?" I said, trying to mask my disappointment and raise some enthusiasm in myself about this date.

"I thought we'd go grab a burger and then come back here to get to know each other better."

"Sounds good," I said, while wondering what he meant by getting to know each other better. I reasoned with myself that he must want to talk with me without Matt around. Maybe he really wanted to get to know me. Maybe he really liked me, and this could be something more than casual?

"Give me a sec and we'll head out."

"Sure." I said with a bright smile plastered on my face. It felt fake, but I was trying. Heck, I'd been such a poor judge with guys so far, maybe there could be something here and I just didn't see it yet. I figured it couldn't hurt to try. We headed out and ordered our burgers with minimal conversation. I still felt uncomfortable inside and was busy trying to come up with conversation starters to ease the feeling.

What little conversation there was centered on Frank and his interest in motor-cross racing, fishing, and flashy cars. Nothing that was deep or meaningful. Nothing that gave me a clue as to why he had asked me out. It seemed as though the only thing we had in common was Matt.

By the time we finished our dinner and got back to the house, the curiosity was burning in my brain like a fire that could only be extinguished with the answer to why he had asked me out. I had to know. Was it because I had dated Matt? Was he really attracted to me and didn't know how to express it? Why didn't he ask me any questions about me? Why didn't he ask about my son? I knew he knew I had a child. I'd brought him over to their house on a few occasions. Matt adored him. Frank never really seemed interested.

We sat down on the couch and the question jumped out of my mouth before I could stop it. "Why did you ask me out?"

Frank looked at me for a moment, as if weighing his response. "Ever since we met, I wanted to, but Matt asked first."

"Really? You didn't seem to mind when Matt and I were dating. I would've never known." I was really curious how I could've missed the clues. I usually could tell when a guy liked me.

"Yeah really, you crazy! Once Matt told me you two were just friends I knew I could ask."

I smiled, pleased at the compliment that he had waited for me.

"Besides, after hearing Matt talk about the way you kiss, I just had to see what all the fuss was about."

What? Frank and Matt had discussed how I kissed? I found that to be strange, but then I reminded myself that I didn't really understand how male friendships worked. Maybe they talked about this sort of thing all the time.

As I was trying to process this information, Frank leaned in to kiss me. A little startled at the abruptness, I decided to go with it anyway, so I kissed him back. I closed my eyes and pretended I was kissing my future husband.

His lips were soft against mine, and our tongues mingled pleasantly together. His lips left mine and traveled down my neck, producing shivers down my spine. His hands began stroking my back and over my hips. It felt good to be touched, and my blood heated.

Then his hands were on my breasts, and I grabbed his hand in protest.

"Don't pretend with me, princess. You know you want it."

"No! It's too fast." I sputtered.

"I know you put out. You have a kid, so no need to act all innocent with me," he sneered.

He grabbed my hands and held them over my head. I tried to pull free, but those muscles I'd admired just hours before held me fast. He pulled up my shirt and roughly squeezed my breast, pinching my nipple until it peaked.

My body went rigid. My mind overcame my reality with old memories, co-mingling with the present. Another pair of hands rubbing my body overlaid Frank's hands in my mind. These hands were old, wrinkled with yellowing nails, and smelled of pipe tobacco.

I no longer fought back. I just lay there un-moving as my mind flooded with the memories of my grandfather touching my young body of nine years. Flashes of Frank removing my pants and underwear mixed in. His hands on my now eighteen-year-old body, acting as though I wanted this, intent on getting his satisfaction.

My mind spun away as Frank shoved himself inside me. I barely registered the pain as he continued to move, pleasuring himself inside my unprepared vagina. He didn't seem to care that I wasn't moving or participating. He was only intent on getting his needs met.

The memories of my grandfather molesting me overlapped with the reality of Frank now date-raping me held me immobile. Trying to protect my soul, my mind went blank. I physically became numb. I could no longer feel what Frank was doing. I felt nothing.

Frank finished and got up, releasing my hands. He left the room and the cold finally registered on my body. I realized I was alone and began pulling my clothes back into place with robotic motions. I heard the shower turn on as I grabbed my purse and moved to the door.

My skin was crawling as though there were small bugs climbing all over my body, and I quietly closed the door behind me and fumbled for my keys. I could feel the bugs' tiny legs marching over my skin, causing me to shake and my skin to chill. The more feeling that returned to my body the more my stomach felt as though I was standing on a high cliff looking over the edge, rolling with nausea. My wrists felt bruised and my shoulders ached. I felt dirty, used, and ashamed. Praying it was just a horrible dream, I climbed behind the wheel and drove home.

As I stood in the scalding shower, trying to scrub away the feeling of creepy crawlies on my flesh, I had flashes of memories invade my mind. Frank's hands, my grandfather's hands, the smell of them, their faces now ugly and interchangeable in my mind.

It's your fault, my mind sinisterly whispered. *You didn't even try to stop it.* Shame burned through my body as I saw myself just lying there, numb, not fighting to stop what was happening.

"I said no," I whispered brokenly to the water, sliding away down the drain, wishing I could follow it.

The next morning, my mother took one look at my pale, tear-stained face, and began asking me what had happened.

"Why are you so upset? Are you hurt?" Her questions bulleted my brain in rapid fire.

"I need to tell you something," I said, my voice coming out in a weak whisper.

"What have you done now?"

Not sure how to tell her, I just blurted it out. "Grandpa molested me!"

"What? When? What are you talking about?" She acted confused, because we hadn't been to their house in quite a while. It did register in my mind that she seemed to know which grandpa I was talking about, even though I hadn't clarified which one. Did she know it was always a possibility?

"It actually happened a long time ago, but I blocked it out."

"I thought I protected you better than that."

"Protected me? You knew? You knew that he might do that?"

"He's done it before, so I always knew he might try. That's why I watched you so closely when we were there."

"Well, I guess not close enough!" I retorted, feeling betrayed. "Why didn't you warn me?"

"We thought he wouldn't do anything with us around. When was this anyway?"

"I think I was nine," I said, letting the tears fall for that little girl who I had been.

"Well, it was a long time ago. We can't do anything about it now," she said and went back to baking as if the conversation hadn't taken place.

I stood stunned, rooted in place as if my feet had been nailed to the floor. That was it? That was the only reaction I would get? No prosecution of the dirty old man? No offer of help or support? No outrage?

Of course not! My old friend the cynic piped up. *You can't prove anything. No one believes you, and you don't deserve to be defended, anyway.*

Feeling small and defeated, I escaped to my room. It hurt my heart to know that revealing the evil done to me had netted me nothing. It would be swept under the rug, never to be talked about. Life would go on as though nothing had happened to me. It was ugly; therefore, no one could know about it.

I swept the date rape under that same rug. With the sting of betrayal fresh in my heart, I built a wall around my soul and placed that wounded little child within it. I would protect her, even if no one else would. I wanted to make sure that no one would be able to touch her, to know her, to betray her ever again.

CHAPTER 7

DESPERATE LOVE

Four years later found me with two kids, pregnant and on the verge of divorce, and that desperate feeling once again. That same feeling of desperation had driven me from my parents' home straight into the arms of Jack, my husband. Now it seemed to be driving me to be alone.

Four years earlier I had left my parents' home because life there had become unbearable to me. The things that had been swept under the rug made me want to avoid the rug all together. Those things were always there, lurking like a dark shadow, whispering how worthless I must be if my own parents could ignore what had happened. I didn't want to live in the same house with people who wouldn't stand up for me, fight for me, and believe in me.

I couldn't afford to move out on my own with my baby. Making minimum wage didn't cut it, and I had no friends willing to room with a baby. Marrying my way out seemed to be the only glimmer of hope for me.

With that faint ray of hope held fast in my mind, I met Jack. He was the newest bouncer at the El Dorado, a nightclub for those eighteen and over that my friends and I frequented.

Jack stood at five foot ten with a slender build, dark blonde hair, and the sweetest blue eyes I had ever seen. His mustache curled playfully over his lip when he flashed his seemingly shy smile.

Throughout the night, I made sure I danced where he could see me, occasionally allowing my eyes to connect with his. When they did, I would grin a little deeper and then look away.

Toward the end of the evening, while I was sipping on my cranberry juice, Jack approached me.

"Are you coming here tomorrow?" he asked while shuffling his feet. I thought it was cute that he seemed so shy.

"I was thinking about it" I responded. Of course, my friends and I were there as often as possible, but he didn't know that.

"Well, if you do, come talk to me. I get off at 11:00 and would like to buy you a drink."

"Alright." I flashed a grin at him and then turned back to my girlfriends. As he walked away, I was busy getting my friends' thoughts and feelings on Jack.

"Oooo! He's cute!"

"He's obviously into you."

"Are you going to go for it?"

"You'd better snag him before someone else does."

I chuckled as they echoed what was going through my own head.

The next night, I let Jack buy me that drink, and almost before I could blink, we were in a relationship. Details are fuzzy exactly how it happened, but it seemed like we talked about it, and then it was happening.

The same thing happened two months later, when I moved in with him and his roommate. Jack was so laidback that I felt completely in control. He gave me the opportunity to move my son and myself out of my parents' home, and I grabbed onto that with both hands.

The next thing I knew, I was planning our wedding. If pressed, I couldn't tell you how or when he proposed. I don't think he could either. Like the rest of our relationship, it just seemed that when we discussed something, it was assumed it was happening and that was it.

I told my friends and family the same story I told myself about our relationship. In my mind it was completely romantic—love at first sight, couldn't stand to be apart, loved my son as if he were his own.

We had a large, fairytale-type wedding. Five bridesmaids and five groomsmen; professional invitations, invited over 150 people, most of whom I didn't even know; announcement in the paper; old-fashioned wedding dress; and more. You would've thought I'd be over-the-moon- happy with it all. Instead, I found myself feeling like the wedding wasn't really mine. It was what everyone told me it was supposed to be.

I was told I had to invite relatives I had never met—I did. I was told I had to invite friends of my parents who I didn't really know—I did. I was told I had to say certain vows—I did. I was told I had to play certain music—I did. When it came time for the reception, Jack and I had a limo take us to my parents' house where we were holding the reception in their backyard. On the way there, I asked the limo driver to take the long way, as I thought it would be romantic to spend some private moments with my new husband. The driver honored my request, and the normal thirty-minute drive took an hour.

When we arrived, my mother stood in the driveway and barked at me "Where have you been? Everyone is here waiting for you."

With my eyes rolling back in my head, I responded, "Gee, sorry. I thought it was my wedding day and it would be romantic to spend some time with my husband."

"It's rude to keep everyone waiting. You can be alone later," she quipped and turned on her heel to march back to the house.

Now embarrassed and feeling as though I was once again wrong, I slowly followed her with Jack close behind me. Would I ever get anything right?

I even found myself thinking of Ken that day. I had invited him to the wedding. Not surprising, he didn't show. I had hand-delivered the invitation to him at the pizza place where he was working at and met his new girlfriend. She didn't seem all that thrilled to meet me. I had thought any worries would be diffused by the fact that I was there to invite him to my wedding. Not so, given that he had told her all about me. Besides, I think she suspected my secret dream.

Some part of me that I was trying desperately to ignore wanted Ken to protest the marriage. I wanted him to realize that I had moved on and that he didn't want me to. In my dreams, I saw him stopping the wedding and professing his undying love to me. In reality, I was acting as if that was the farthest thought in my head. I wanted so much to really be over him, but I didn't know if I ever would be. I thought marrying Jack would help me.

It wasn't very long before the one-bedroom apartment we shared with Jack's roommate got way too small. Sleeping on the pull-out bed with Ben in the crib next to us just wasn't cutting it, not to mention I was constantly exhausted as I was working full-time and coming home to do all the cleaning and cooking. It seemed that all the guys did was play video games and make a mess. Something needed to change, so we moved to Manteca to live with his parents while we saved to get our own place.

While living with his parents, I learned a lot more about the man I had married. He seemed content to have his mom take complete care of him. She did all the cooking, cleaning, and laundry. I tried to contribute, but it seemed that once again, no matter what I did, it was wrong, or not enough. It was stifling, to say the least. I felt the pressure to get out of there and make our own home. Jack seemed in no hurry, though.

I found myself nagging at him to find work and constantly talking about having a baby together. I had it firmly in my mind that when we got our own place and had a baby, I would be happy at last.

Eventually we did find our own place and I did get pregnant. I was over-the-moon excited. I rode that wave of happiness for all it was worth until it all went horribly wrong.

I hadn't been feeling well, and it kept nagging in the back of my mind that something wasn't right. I did the best I could to ignore that feeling by trying out baby names and dreaming about having that happily-ever-after—finally.

At the doctor's office for my regular prenatal checkup, I lay back on the table with the sheet of paper they stretch out on the table crinkling beneath me. I exposed my belly and tried not to hold my breath as the doctor jolted my skin with that cold stethoscope checking my heartbeat, which was rapidly pounding away. He murmured "good" and moved the stethoscope down to my five-months-pregnant, rounded belly.

His bushy grey eyebrows knit together as he moved the stethoscope in different spots, and a slight frowned marked his face. I swallowed hard, blocking the question of *What's wrong?* that had leaped to my throat. He began asking me about the baby's movement and told the nurse to set up an ultrasound.

No words were spoken during the ultrasound. There was only an ugly, heavy intensity weighing in the air. After it was over and I sat uncomfortably on that paper-covered table that crackled loudly with each slight movement, I wrapped my arms around my bulging stomach and waited for the doctor to speak.

"I'm sorry to tell you that we were unable to find a heartbeat for the baby," he stated in a quiet voice. At that proclamation, I went numb. I sat there, an unmoving blob, holding my waist as if to hold onto that little soul that was no longer there. As my mind swam through the sludge that it seemed to be drowning in, I vaguely registered the doctor telling me I would have to come back, that they would abort the now-dead fetus. I nodded my head that I understood and slowly slipped from the table.

When I got home and told my husband, I received little reaction. He seemed more concerned about whether he needed to take time off of work to care for me after the procedure than the fact that our child had died. To me it felt that a part of me had been ripped from my soul. I couldn't comprehend his lack of feeling.

After the procedure, I stuffed my emotions further inside and began searching for ways to fill the aching hole that now resided in my heart. I talked about writing a book. I was told I would never get it published, so what was the point? I asked for more hours at work and was told they weren't available. I begged for a puppy and was told no—that I was only trying to replace the baby. I scoffed at such things, for I knew I could never replace that little lost soul.

I wondered what I had done to make her decide not to be here with me on this earth. I wondered why it seemed as though the universe was conspiring to keep my happily-ever-after from me.

After a few months, I decided it was time to try again. I desperately wanted a baby. I got my wish. This time I had a successful pregnancy, even though during this pregnancy we decided to move back to Sacramento. Even though my husband moved there before me, as he had a job there. Even though I had to constantly drive there with my five-year-old son and my enlarged, uncomfortable belly to find us a place to live. I never could understand why he couldn't find us a place when he was living there. And even though I had to pack our entire house and get my friends and family to help us move because he was too busy with work, I had a successful pregnancy.

On her due date, Jack decided to go out with his friends. I was worried, because I knew the time was close for our daughter to arrive. I repeatedly made sure he would check in frequently and that someone had a phone I could call if I went into labor.

Later that day, waiting for my husband and his friends to come home, I went into labor. I had girlfriends over, so I wasn't alone, and I knew that he would be home anytime. They had said that they would be gone only a few hours, and that had long since passed—not to mention that he had not checked in once.

Getting to the point where I didn't think I could wait much longer, I had my friend try to call the number they'd left with us. She left several voicemails. We never received a call back. Finally, my friends drove me to the hospital, leaving one last message for the guys that we were on our way there.

Later, I would find out that his friends had taken him to a strip club and they never heard the phone ringing. I wasn't happy about it but wrote it off as boys being boys. I had more important things to worry about anyway.

After our daughter, Leyna, was born, they whisked her away from me before I got to hold her. After tests and assurances, we found out that she had a hole between two of the chambers in her heart. They told us it was minor and that she would just need to be monitored.

Later, we found that the hole would require surgery to place a patch in her heart. As we were dealing with the reality of our baby daughter having open heart surgery, our marriage crumbled even more, and the gap between us widened.

I was working full time and coming home to find the house a mess, the kids to care for, and my husband playing video games and having his friends over on a constant basis. I was worn out and tired of fighting to make it all change. I felt completely abandoned and alone. Thoughts of escape constantly drove my daydreams. I wanted out.

I didn't know how to get out, so I continued on mechanically, dragging through each day. Sex between us had always been infrequent, and now I didn't want it at all. One night, as I lay in bed, my back resolutely to him, I felt his hand begin rubbing my arm. At first I didn't respond, but then curiosity began to grow. I had always been the initiator before. Were things finally changing? I had to know if the possibility to save this marriage was there. After all, we had two kids together and I really did want it to work.

I gathered my energy and turned toward my husband, responding now to his caresses. I did my best to stuff down the feeling of numbness, like I wasn't truly in my body. I was trying to recapture how I used to feel when he touched me. I was never able to get there. By the time he finished, I was done—done with the marriage. I knew it in my core, and there were no longer any lingering doubts in my mind. I had done everything I knew to make it work. Now I just had to figure out how to get out of the marriage while ensuring my kids were taken care of.

A couple of months passed while I was secretly exploring my options. He didn't touch me again. I think part of him knew it was over as well. I was stressed and hadn't been feeling well. I figured it was just the stress, then one day I realized I hadn't gotten my period! *No! It's not possible*, the voice in my head screamed, *I can't be pregnant!* My mind began churning over all the symptoms I had been experiencing that told me I was. Nausea, check. Appetite changes, check. No period, check. Emotional, check. Feeling the need to panic, check.

I bought a pregnancy test on the way home from work that day, and upon arriving home immediately went into the bathroom to take it. I tuned out the fact that my husband was downstairs with his friends, once again playing video games, expecting me to cook for them. I paced anxiously in the tiny bathroom, staring at the soft, dark green rug as my feet made impressions, sinking into it. Glancing between the pictures of wildflowers, my watch, and the test, I waited to see if the blue line would appear or remain clear in the allotted time. The test said it could take up to ten minutes for the results, but within two minutes there was a solid blue line—positive. I sank down to the bathroom floor, stunned. How could this be? We hadn't been together for months, and the last time we were I had just finished my period, so I shouldn't have been able to get pregnant. Now what was I going to do? How could I leave with a six-year-old, an infant that needed heart surgery, and a baby in my belly? I felt trapped.

I slowly walked down the carpeted stairs of our townhouse and up to Jack. "Surprise!" I said with a false smile on my face as I thrust the damning pregnancy test under his nose. He glanced down at it and shoved my hand back.

"Your fault, your problem," he said with a sneer and turned back to his game. My cheeks turned red as I felt anger flush my skin. His friends made a point not to look at me, and the silence was suffocating.

"That's funny," I retorted, "I don't remember being there alone." I turned on my heel and went to the kitchen to begin preparing dinner.

The next couple of months I lived purely on autopilot. I worked, came home, cooked, and cleaned. I slept. I got up and did it all again. The only breaks in the monotonous routine were the prenatal visits and the doctor visits, which ensured the coming baby was healthy. I also tried to determine just how critical our daughter's need for heart surgery was. Communication between my husband and me was sparse, with the doctor visits being one of the few topics we could discuss without arguing. Even with my living in survival mode, it seemed to be a foregone conclusion that I was staying because I was pregnant.

Then we got the call that our daughter's heart surgery had finally been scheduled at Stanford University. After making arrangements for Ben's care, we made the drive with Leyna to Palo Alto, California. Silence reigned as we drove, my head crowded with my hopes and fears for our little girl. I felt completely alone as the wheels sped over the pavement, even though my husband was sitting right next to me in the car. The gap between us might as well have been the Grand Canyon with no way to cross.

After checking Leyna in for surgery, we waited in the surgery waiting area. I held onto her and refused to put her down. I constantly talked to her, assuring her she was going to be fine, that I loved her, and this was a good thing. I didn't want her to be scared. After what seemed like hours, the doctor, anesthesiologist, and nurse came to take her in the operating room.

The nurse held up her arms to Leyna as the doctor began explaining what the process and expected time frame would be. Leyna immediately leaned toward the nurse, arms open, with a bright smile on her face. In all of her eight months of life I had never seen her respond that way to anyone but a family member or close friend of the family. Surprised but inwardly feeling a bit of relief that it was a good sign, I reluctantly let her move from my arms to the waiting arms of the nurse.

With a worried but confident heart I slumped onto the yellow couch in the waiting area and pulled out the latest Stephen King novel. It was over seven hundred pages, and I figured it would keep me occupied during the wait for Leyna's surgery to be over. Goodness knows I didn't want to spend it trying to make conversation with Jack.

Alternately reading and staring at the clock, time seemed to drag slower than ever. At hour four of what was to have been a two-hour surgery, the doctor finally came to tell us that the surgery had gone well and that she was in recovery. It would be days before she could come home. I chose to stay with her the entire time.

Sleeping on a sparse cot in the small waiting room at night while pregnant was not physically comfortable; however, the emotional relief of not being in the same house as my husband was like having a huge boulder taken off my shoulders. Focused solely on Leyna's recovery, what tests they were conducting, and when she would be released to go home allowed me to ignore the bigger issue of continuing to live on autopilot. I should have known that the universe wouldn't allow me to avoid reality for long.

The Thanksgiving holiday was looming while I stayed at Stanford with Leyna. I was so exhausted that I didn't want to consider doing anything about it. Then the doctors told me that they expected to release Leyna the day before Thanksgiving. When I told Jack, he told me his family wanted to come to our house for Thanksgiving to celebrate Leyna coming home. I told him I was too exhausted to plan and cook a big dinner and that I thought the house should be quiet and peaceful for Leyna's homecoming. That was the end of the conversation.

Leyna was released on the promised day before Thanksgiving, and we arrived home to a messy but quiet dwelling. With a sigh mixed with disgust at the mess I now had to clean, I felt relief that I didn't have to deal with a house full of people. I began getting Leyna settled in. Jack leaned in the doorway, nervously clearing his throat. I turned to him with one eyebrow raised "What?"

"Ummm—I just wanted to let you know my family is coming here for dinner tomorrow."

"What?" I exclaimed, sure I had heard him wrong.

"You don't have to do anything," he stammered, "They're bringing everything, and Mom said she'd take care of all the cooking and cleaning."

Stunned that he had directly gone against what we had discussed and angry that he seemed to completely disregard what I needed, I replied through clenched teeth, "I specifically told you that I was too tired for this. I can't believe you did this."

"It's not that big a deal," he pleaded. "I said you don't have to lift a finger."

But for me it was a big deal. For me it was the last straw. I knew with a certainty in my soul that things between us would never get better. Heck, they wouldn't even stay where I could live in autopilot. They were only getting worse. Two children and pregnant or not, I had to get out.

That night I began sleeping in my daughter's room on the spare bed. Even though we hadn't been intimate for quite awhile, the thought of sleeping in the same room with him turned my stomach. After a few nights of this, Jack realized I had no intention of ever sleeping in the same bed with him again. The gap was widening, and to me it had become insurmountable.

I had lain down on the small twin bed, trying to get comfortable with my swollen stomach and the baby moving around inside, when Jack's frame filled the doorway. "Oh, no! You're not sleeping in here again," he spat from his mouth.

"Quiet! You'll wake up Leyna." I hissed. She was sleeping peacefully in the crib snug against the wall opposite the bed where I laid.

He lowered his voice, but the anger still resonated through

"You are to get back into our room right now. I'm not putting up with this any longer."

"I'm staying right here. Now go away. I'm tired and need to go to sleep."

Instead of verbally replying, he did something he had never done before. He strode into the room, anger radiating off of him, and washing over me. His hand snaked out, grabbed me by the wrist, and dragged me from the bed. I landed on the floor with a thud, twisting to protect the baby I was carrying. Shocked at his physical manhandling, I tried to pull my arm back.

He tightened his grip and began dragging me across the floor toward our room across the hall. "Let go!" I demanded in as forceful a whisper as I dared. I did not want Leyna to awaken and see her father dragging me across the floor by my wrist. Nor did I want Ben, sleeping in the room right next door, to witness his mother being physically abused.

He ignored my demand and continued to drag my unwilling body. As we began to pass the stairway I gained my footing and dug my heels in to halt his progress. At that point, some dark part of me had the fleeting thought to kick him down the stairs. The image of his body falling backwards down the stairs, coming to rest at the bottom, broken and unmoving, flitted through my mind.

Instead, I pulled back my free arm and bunched my fist tightly. It connected to his body square in the middle of his chest with a loud smacking sound. Stunned, he dropped my wrist to rub where his chest was quickly turning red. "Ow! That hurt." He looked at me accusingly.

Holding my injured wrist where the bruising was already starting to appear in the shape of his fingers, I spat back, "That was just a warning shot. Don't you ever touch me like that again. Next time I will kill you."

As he looked at me in disbelief, I turned on my heel and marched back into Leyna's room, praying he would leave me alone. The days following were full of careful avoidance and terse silence. The round bruise in the middle of his chest and the finger-shaped ones on my wrists played as vivid reminders that all was not well in our home.

A week later, we were notified that the townhouse we were living in was being sold. This was my golden opportunity, and I grabbed on with both hands. "What are we going to do?" Jack asked when I showed him the letter. "I guess we can start looking for a new place."

Drawing a deep breath of courage, I replied, "I think this is the time for you to get your own place and I'll get mine."

After a moment of confused silence, he said, "What do you mean?"

"We're not getting any better, and I feel it's time we went our separate ways."

"I thought things were fine. We haven't been fighting or anything. There must be someone else," he lashed out.

"We haven't been fighting because I've been too exhausted from having the same argument over and over. There is no one else—I'm not a cheater." I replied heatedly. I couldn't believe he thought that I would do that. I'm not saying the thought didn't cross my mind, and Lord knows I had opportunities. I just knew that it was a path I never wanted to go down.

"Yeah, right!" he spat back, "Whatever!" and turned his back to me, effectively ending the conversation once again. There was really nothing left to say anyway, as far as I was concerned.

Pregnant and two small children on my own. Could I really do this?

CHAPTER 8

ROUGH EDGES

I managed to find a house to rent along with a roommate. As stressful as the move was, it was everyone telling me how stupid I was being that far surpassed it by leaps and bounds. No one seemed to believe that I could raise three kids on my own. No one seemed to understand why I had to leave instead of staying in misery. The more they told me I couldn't or I shouldn't, the angrier I became. I was on my way to having three children; I didn't need a fourth. And that's what my husband had become to me—a fourth child.

It was exhausting living in the land of anger and resentment, and my friends were falling to the wayside fast and furious. I knew that anger wasn't good for the baby I was carrying, let alone for my kids who were already here. The problem was that I needed a healthy outlet for it, and I had no idea what that could be. What I really wanted was revenge.

Throughout the day and especially as I lay in bed at night, I would spin fantasies in my head of the different ways I could exact revenge on all those who had hurt me, betrayed me, and abandoned me.

As my ex-husband stayed stagnant, working a low-end job, playing video games and pining away for me, I would raise my three children to be happy, healthy, successful human beings. I would become very successful in my own right and never again have financial problems. I would meet and marry a handsome, successful man who would treat me like a goddess, and we would be wildly happy. Those who had abandoned and betrayed me would want to get back into my circle of friends but would be denied. They would live with regret for not having cherished what they had when they had me.

These were the common dreams that I longed for. The end result of the "revenge" scenario was always the same. Me—happy. I had often heard that the best revenge is to be happy. I didn't really know if it was even possible, but damn, I wanted to try.

If I could help and fix all those other people who had come to me over the years, I could certainly fix myself. What would I say to someone who had all my problems?

Ha! my inner critic smirked, *You're such a mess. You'll never get it together.*

"Fine!" I replied back with stubborn determination, "Then I'll start by getting it together."

Organizing I could do. I was innately good at it. I liked things a certain way, and everything had a place. I found it soothing to eliminate chaos whenever possible by planning as much as possible. Unfortunately, with two small children and one more on the way, plans rarely worked out the way I thought they should.

It was hard enough to get them fed, clothed, clean, and off to daycare or school while I held down my job, let alone keep the house clean and organized. My roommate wasn't much help in this arena, either.

One thing I could do, and desperately wanted to do, was to get the divorce finalized. I had told Jack that he could visit the kids whenever he wanted and to figure out what he could afford to pay for child support. Three months had passed and he had only seen the kids once and had paid very little. This was not going to work. I no longer wanted to be in a relationship with him, but I did want him to have a relationship with the kids. I would never take their father from them. I also wanted to provide a decent living for them, and I felt strongly that he should contribute to that.

So, I began documenting everything—visits, phone conversations, child support, or lack thereof, in preparation of getting it finalized. I studied and prepared the divorce papers myself, as I couldn't afford to pay an attorney.

One day, as I was venting to a coworker about all the paperwork involved when filing for divorce, I also railed about how I had been victimized all my life and now felt like this was just another victimization. She asked me a life-altering question. "Have you ever heard of codependency?"

"No. Why?" I responded, while in my head I was wondering what the heck that had to do with everything I'd just told her. She was supposed to help me to fix myself, not ask me strange questions.

"Well, I read this book a while back and I think you should read it. It's about codependency, and from what you've told me, I think it might help you."

"Are you saying I'm codependent?" I asked, not sure whether or not to be offended.

"No. I'm just saying I think it might help you. Codependency is about people who are so busy helping everyone else that they lose themselves in the process. I could be wrong, but it sounds like what you've described to me. Just check it out. It's called *Codependent No More* by Melody Beattie."

I shrugged my shoulders. Why not? Who knows? It could help.

"Alright. Thanks," I said aloud and then wrote down the author and title so I wouldn't forget it when I went to the bookstore to find it later that day.

That book was like an awakening for me. I had been raised to always put others first, ignore my own needs, and that the only way to be considered a good person was to always help others, no matter what. This is why I drove myself to exhaustion, fixing their problems while ignoring my own. I so desperately wanted to be liked and considered good, and I had been told that this was the only way to happiness.

I devoured the book, taking the self-evaluations and reading through it in one night. I was excited to realize that I had found some answers at long last. That gaping hole I had always felt in my heart and soul was tingling with the possibility of closure.

Helping others did make me feel good and self-satisfied, at least for a little while. Helping others had become like alcohol to me. It numbed my own pain and made me feel intoxicatingly good for a period of time. But just like an alcoholic, it never lasted for long and was never enough. I always wanted more. Besides, whenever I turned to anyone else for help, they were never there for me. When was it my turn?

Of course, even broaching the question of *When was it my turn?* in my head brought up feelings of guilt and selfishness. What a vicious cycle.

Codependent No More showed that I was supposed to have both. Taking care of others and myself, and that unless I did this I would burn out and then no longer be able to help anyone.

In order to take care of myself, I needed to learn what made me happy, who helped me grow, who supported me, and clear the path of those who were unsupportive or held me back. It was time to clean my inner house.

I started with the most obvious tasks first. Getting those divorce papers in. I had been procrastinating filing them, trying to be nice to Jack and getting nowhere. I wrote out the visitation agreement the way I felt it needed to be and then left it up to the court to determine how much child support he should pay. I had them completed and filed within the week.

Once that was underway, I cleaned house—the literal one. I had long felt that your literal house reflects your inner one, and I was tired of mine being dirty and cluttered. I began preparations for the baby on the way, making the call list for when I went into labor and readying the crib.

The divorce finalized, and shortly after, Adam came along on March 7, a healthy, big baby boy. As a matter of fact, he was larger than they had told me I could have—a full one and a half pounds larger. After he was born and they brought him to me, I asked how much he weighed. When they told me that he weighed eight pounds, five ounces, I was shocked. I was only supposed to be able to birth a seven-pounder max. I looked at my doctor and promptly said, "Don't ever tell me I can't do something again."

He just laughed, but that became my new life motto. If someone told me I couldn't do something, like raising three kids on my own and being happy, I would show them by exceeding all expectations. I was going to get revenge, come hell or high water.

Six weeks later I had lost all the baby weight and decided to have a party. I invited those few remaining friends who had stayed supportive of me, and my mother. I wanted a better relationship with her, and I thought this would be a good start. I was determined to no longer accept negativity from anyone, and this night was to be about girls getting together and celebrating.

The party was going along great. Everyone seemed to be having a good time. The house had stayed clean and I felt good about myself, especially after discovering I could fit into all my pre-pregnancy clothes and it had only been six weeks. It had taken me six months to lose all the weight with the first pregnancy and three months for the second one. Cutting that time in half once again was something in and of itself to celebrate.

As the party was winding down, I sat down to take a break from hostess duties and began to listen in on the conversation taking place between my mother and my guests.

"Oh, I know she thinks she can handle it, but I don't see how she can. She was such a terrible, willful child, and I'm sure her children will be the same way," my mother said to the group.

My ears didn't register the murmured responses from my friends as I sat in shock. I had extended my hand in friendship and it got bit. How dare she come into my home and insult me to my friends. The smoldering anger was quickly building as I tuned back into her as she continued to speak, oblivious to the explosion building within me.

"I mean, I can't believe that she thinks it's better to be divorced and struggle with these babies. They are the ones who will suffer; mark my words. It was bad enough that she was a teenage mother; now this."

As the looks of sympathy from my friends turned toward me, I decided it was time for action. I got my mother's coat from the back room where it lay on my twin bed, snug against the wall to make room for the two cribs, one for Leyna and one for Adam. I handed it to my mother and said that I would walk her out. By unspoken agreement no one else left the house, giving me the time alone with my mother that I needed.

In the past, I had always internalized her negative comments, trying to rationalize that she meant well. It had only fed my negative self-talk, and I considered it to be one of the obstacles to my happiness. It was time for me to respond differently if I wanted it to change.

"I invited you tonight because I wanted to include you in celebrating with me. I wanted a better relationship with you. Instead, you came in to my home and proceeded to tell everyone what a terrible child I was and how you think I'm just a big screw-up."

"I didn't mean—," was barely out of her mouth before I cut her off. I was on a roll, actually saying what I wanted to say, and I wasn't about to stop.

"It doesn't matter what you meant. Fact is, I will not be disrespected like that in my own home in front of my friends and children. You are no longer welcome here. I want nothing more to do with you. If I'm such a screw-up, then you don't need to be around me. I can take care of my kids myself. I don't need you. You will not have contact with my kids or me again, period. Have a good life." I turned on my heel and left her standing in my driveway.

I felt strangely elated at having stood up for myself to my mother. At the same time, I was sad that it had come to this. I just wanted her to love me, accept me, and be proud of me, but it seemed that if I made different choices than she would make, it would make me unlovable to her.

Albeit rough, I had just set the first boundary in my life. Now I had to stand by it.

Six months passed before I spoke to my mother again. My dad had finally intervened when he couldn't take the gap of separation any longer. I had ignored all calls from my mother and refused to go to any family gatherings. I had continued to live and make my way without her, just as I said. While it hurt, it had also been a relief to not have the negativity constantly in my space. Then my dad called.

"This has to stop. Your mother is upset and crying all the time, and I can't live like this anymore." His normal gentle and humorous voice sounded angry and hard over the phone. "You need to apologize and bring this family back together."

"I need to apologize?" I asked, my voice reaching a strained high pitch as I felt that push on the boundary I had set. "Did she tell you what she did?"

"No, and I don't care. I just want this done with."

Standing up to my mom was one thing. Standing up to my dad caused my heart to squeeze painfully as my legs shook. At one time I had been his little girl—until my little brother had come along and seemed to occupy so much of his heart that I no longer knew where I fit in. That part of me that still longed to be his little girl again wanted to acquiesce and sweep it all back under the rug. The newly born part of me that wanted to be strong and happy for once took charge, instead.

"You need to understand what happened. She came over to my home and proceeded to tell my guests what a terrible child I was, what an awful mother she thinks I am, and what a selfish idiot I am. I am tired of all the negativity. I will no longer tolerate it in my life. The only way I will speak to her again is if she apologizes."

He sighed and said, "I understand. I'll talk to her."

As we hung up, I felt calm. I did it. I held my boundary. Yes, I would like to repair my relationship with my mother, but I refused to do it at the cost of myself any longer. I felt like I was finally making progress toward being happy.

My mother did call and apologize a few days later, and we slowly began to rebuild a relationship again. However, this time it felt different. I no longer felt ruled by the need for her acceptance. For her part, she also seemed to understand that something had shifted between us. She made visible efforts to not be negative toward me. The criticisms didn't stop completely, but I could tell that she was more conscientious with me.

With this victory of sorts under my belt, I began to focus on discovering more areas where I needed to set boundaries and to work on smoothing out the rough edges of my newfound skill. I thought I had it licked by the time I met Mark.

CHAPTER 9

REVENGE IS SWEET

After making the break from Mark, and having my parents move him in while I was left alone, facing bankruptcy, I knew in my gut it was time to get my revenge. They were going to pay in misery, and I never wanted to find myself back in this type of situation again. I was going to be happy, damn it.

I had thought I'd recovered from my codependency, but based on my relationship with Mark, it was now obvious to me that I had not. I was still attracting the same kind of man. The needy ones, the ones I secretly wanted to fix. It was so much easier for me to overlook the warning signs in the beginning of relationships.

"Oh, that's just a little thing. It'll change later," I would always reassure myself. Later would only reveal that the little thing had, in fact, become a big, huge thing, and something I could no longer live with or overlook.

Men might as well have been alien creatures to me. For that matter, in most cases, women were, too. I had very few female friends, as I hated drama and games and could not rationalize their thinking most of the time. Yet, that seemed to be what I drew to me. These were the type of people who constantly showed up and wanted me to "fix" them, give them all the answers. It was easy for me to see ways over, under, around, or through almost any obstacle someone else was facing, and—a bonus—it allowed me to ignore my own issues.

I knew I needed to find a way to stop this pattern, and in order to do that I needed to understand myself and how men and women thought. The first step in changing a pattern is to be aware that there is one. I had that part down. Now I needed to figure out the next step.

One thing I knew about ensuring I no longer fell into the codependency trap again was that I needed to get clearer on what made me happy, what I wanted to attract into my life, and what I would no longer tolerate. I needed to define and hold my personal boundaries with much more clarity, and that would require really getting to know the inner me.

My finances, being in the state of mess that they were, was definitely something I could not ignore or put off—not to mention that it was occupying much of my energy and time. Mark had not only drained our accounts, but he had gone far into debt, and my name was dragged in there with his.

In desperation, I filed for bankruptcy. It seemed to be the only answer to me at the time. I had to do something, as I had three kids to support and feed. Feelings of shame and embarrassment flooded me at the thought that I had to resort to this. The one advantage to my filing was that it forced me to organize all the debts and enabled me to see exactly where I stood with what. Once that happened, I was able to start paying off the numerous minor debts that had piled up and start paying down the larger ones. As the mountain got smaller and smaller, I realized that I really did not need to file the bankruptcy, and I had it dismissed. Getting control of my finances, now that I was the only one on my bank account, cleared the way for me to begin to focus more inward.

This was scary and a relief to me at the same time. I had no idea of what made me happy. I knew I felt good making others happy, but I also needed to figure out, what were the things that made me happy? What was important to me besides the obvious answer of my kids, friends, and work?

Silence was my only answer when I asked myself what would make me happy. My head and my heart seemed to have no answers other than what didn't make me happy. Determined to overcome the perceived obstacle, I decided to start with the information I had—what didn't make me happy.

My looks didn't make me happy. By the time Mark and I divorced, I was overweight. My hair was a frizzy mess, and I was wearing unattractive glasses because I was unable to buy myself contacts when he was constantly draining the money. When I looked in the mirror, I saw a big ball of frumpy unhappiness. I was just a plain mess, nothing hot left about me. This had to change.

I did remember how much I used to enjoy going out to the local bar, where I had met Mark, and dancing. I hadn't danced in so long that I wasn't sure I remembered how, and with the way I was looking, I was sure no one

My heart had given a little leap when I saw him. I released the breath I didn't know I was holding and turned back to my friend. "Well, tell him I'd be happy to dance with him; anything but a slow dance, because I'm with someone."

"Right!" my friend said as he gave me a wink and sauntered off in the direction the tall drink of water had disappeared to. That sexy guy had piqued my interest, but he never did approach for that wanted dance that night.

The next few months consisted of more of Eric letting me down and being unresponsive to the relationship and my needs, while the mysterious stranger and I shared flirtatious looks and smiles. He still didn't approach me to dance, though. He would just watch as I danced or dance near me but never right next to me. Whenever our eyes would meet I'd smile or wink, and he'd grin and then look away.

After weeks of not even getting a phone call, I finally I knew that my time with Eric was done, and I called him to arrange the exchange of our items that had crept into each other's homes. The slow death of our relationship had allowed me to grieve it already, and I no longer felt sad about it. I was just ready.

It was a Friday night, and I got ready to go dancing. I'd be stopping by Eric's on the way to exchange our stuff, and then I was going out. I looked good and felt more like myself than I had for the last several months. I felt no ill will toward Eric. I was ready to let him go with love.

When I pulled in front of his house, he met me at the curb. He had the microwave I had loaned him when his burned out sitting near his feet, and a slight frown marred his brow.

I got out of the car with a smile and opened the trunk of my little green Saturn car. After he silently put my microwave in the trunk, he shut it and turned toward me with a look of confusion. "You're going out?" he asked in disbelief as his eyes took in my outfit.

"Yeah, why not? I've done enough sitting around and grieving over our relationship for the last month. I'm ready to have some fun. No hard feelings, though. I wish you the best," I quipped as I gave him a quick hug and turned to go.

Seemingly stunned and unsure of how to respond, he half-hugged me back and stepped back on the curb with his eyebrows still knit together. I'm sure he had never had such an easy break-up. I know I hadn't. I felt so healthy and grounded. I knew I had made the right decision as I drove to the bar. This was definitely the ultimate revenge—happiness!

While driving, I decided that it would be a while before I'd date again. For now, I just wanted to enjoy life. Almost immediately upon arriving at the bar, the universe put that to the test.

A guy who I had talked with several times approached me to dance. During the dance and conversation, he found out that I was newly single and promptly asked me out. I considered him for a moment before answering. He was five foot nine, blonde and blue-eyed with a sweet smile. He had always been very sweet, and at any other time I would have been interested, but I had just made a promise to myself and I intended to keep it.

"Sorry," I replied. "I just got out of a relationship and don't want to date for a while."

"I understand," he stated, reaffirming my belief that he was sweet. "Just let me know when you're ready to date again, and I'm first in line."

I laughed and we parted as I went back to my table to quench my thirst.

I was standing at the bistro-style table, leaning on it, sipping my beer and watching as the dancers two-stepped in a whirling circle around the floor. My foot tapped quietly in rhythm to the beat while I just enjoyed the moment of feeling happy with who I was and my life.

In the peripheral of my eye I caught a movement, and I turned away from the dancers on the floor to find that tall drink-of-water my friend had previously pointed out to me. He was leaning on my table.

"Hi!" he said with a wickedly sexy little grin.

"Hi, yourself." I said as a dozen questions flitted through my mind. *Why had he not talked to me before, after the multitude of exchanged smiles and winks? What made him approach me tonight? Who was he? Why did my heart speed up just at his presence? What would he say next?*

"So—," he drawled out, "Can I ask you something?"

"Umm, sure."

"How come your old man is never in here with you?"

"There is no old man anymore," the words popped out of my mouth without thought. His face lit up at that answer, and he introduced himself as Dave. He shared that he worked in construction and appeared pleasantly surprised that I was, too, although in a different capacity than he was. It was nice to have a conversation with someone where I didn't have to explain construction terms to them when I was describing something at work, like what a glulam was.

Dave was a carpenter and I was a safety professional. It was kind of surprising that our paths hadn't crossed on a job site somewhere before, yet I was would ask me anyway, but I figured I could at least learn to line dance in the meantime, as dancing was good exercise and a way for me to start to take off the weight.

During the next few months, I'd find a sitter as often as I could and go to the bar. I focused on learning the line dances and tried not to care that the guys I found attractive would pass their eyes over me as if I wasn't even there. How different it was from a few years before when I'd met Mark there.

I eventually acquired contacts and got my hair frizz under control. It seemed that the more I learned to dance, the more free I felt. Dancing became my outlet. My confidence grew as the weight began to slip off, and I truly started feeling like a whole person in my own right. And something else I noticed—the happier I became with myself, the more the "hotties" seemed to be attracted to me.

I wasn't out searching for a relationship with anyone. I was determined that the only relationships I would focus on for a while were the ones with my kids—and with myself. But that didn't mean I couldn't have fun exploring those fascinating creatures called men and what made them tick.

While trying to figure out men and women's thought processes, and how I fit into it all, I stumbled across a book by John Gray, *Men are from Mars and Women are from Venus*. What a revelation that was. Men and women are aliens.

John Gray's book enabled me to understand why I responded the way I did to things men did or said, and why they responded the way they did to me. I used his book to review my past relationships, trying to dissect where I went wrong in each. I learned which choices I had made, mostly the ones from a codependent place which led to my repeating a self-defeating pattern instead of overcoming it.

Now that I had clarity around my part, I could work on forgiving myself and letting it go. I also had a better idea of what boundaries I needed to set in place around relationships

My focus became enjoying my family, friends, dancing, reading, and work. I felt freer, lighter, and more anchored in my body. I delved more into my spirituality, reveling in the freedom to explore what felt right and true to me without someone telling me I was crazy or wrong. I made a practice of grounding myself daily, and learning to take care of myself as well as others by getting massages, taking time just for me, and generally doing things I enjoyed.

I dated a bit but kept it casual. This enabled me to drop the relationship whenever there were warning signs that going further would be falling back into my old pattern—that is, until Eric. Something about him swept me out of casual and into wanting more. I chased him and caught him, yet never felt like I truly held him. Even though this was contrary to what I learned in *Men are from Mars, Women are from Venus*, I ignored that and told myself that this relationship was the exception. On the surface, it appeared to be working out fine.

We spent time together. Our families mixed well. He treated me well—or so it seemed. There was something missing, however; something elusive. I couldn't put my finger on it, but it seemed that when we got close, he would pull back. I did my best to let go of trying to control how and where the relationship was going by continuing to live my independence.

I still went dancing by myself. Eric didn't dance, but I had plenty of friends there, so I was never truly alone. Everyone knew I was in a relationship, and that helped to keep it friendly without getting hit on all the time. I knew the bartenders well, and they helped to keep an eye out for me.

This pattern had continued for some time when I began to feel discontented. I was not happy with the relationship but wasn't quite ready to end it. I had realized that I wasn't asking for what I wanted. Instead, I was just accepting when he let me down. I would shrug it off and try to move on instead of expressing how I felt. A prime example was when he planned a trip to Hawaii, without me, and would be gone for my birthday.

I was upset but did my best to shrug it off. My friends seemed more horrified than I was that he didn't even wish me happy birthday after he returned. I knew it wasn't right, but for some reason I kept struggling along.

A month or so later, one of my male friends approached me after I left the dance floor for a brief break. "Hey! I know someone who wants to dance with you," he said with a mischievous sparkle in his eye.

"Really?" I responded with one eyebrow raised.

"Yep. He's been watching you for a while now and would like to dance with you."

"Well, who is he?" I felt curious in spite of myself.

He turned and pointed across the bar to a man who was definitely a tall drink of water. He was six foot four, with dark brown hair and a sexy handlebar mustache that curled down past his lips. I could see that his build was lanky as he casually leaned against a table, watching the dance floor—until he saw my friend pointing him out to me. Then his face got slightly flushed as he turned away and walked to a place behind other people where I could no longer view him.

secretly grateful that they hadn't. For one, most construction workers didn't appreciate that I was there to keep them safe, and therefore, I wasn't the favorite person at work. Two, I refused to date any guy I worked with. Mixing work and relationships rarely worked out, and I didn't need to add more problems to my plate.

We spent the next several hours sharing our stories and enjoying getting to know things about each other. As we parted he simply asked if I would be there the next night. I affirmed that I would, and we agreed we'd see each other then.

I spent the remainder of the night with a silly little grin on my face and the excitement and anticipation at seeing Dave again racing my heart. My friends who had noticed the hours I spent talking with the tall, sexy drink-of-water teased me about my grin and preoccupied mind, for it was filled with what I would wear, what the next meeting would bring, and how good I felt while talking to him.

The next night we met and spent more time together, during which he asked me to dance. This caused my heart to soar, as one of the things I'd decided on was no more dating any man who did not share my love of dancing. Dancing was freeing. Dancing was a stress reliever. Dancing made me happy, and I wanted someone I could share that with.

As the night drew to a close, he leaned in and said, "Look, I know you just got out of a relationship, and I'm not looking for a relationship either, but Monday is my birthday, and I don't want to eat dinner alone on my birthday. Would you have dinner with me on Monday, just as friends?"

"Well, how can I say no to that? No one should be eating alone on their birthday."

We went to the bar to get a napkin for me to write my number on. Keith, the bartender who always watched out for me, looked at me with a question in his eyes when I asked him for a pen. He knew that I never gave out my number and seemed shocked that I was now doing so. "You sure?" he asked and shrugged, handing me the pen when I nodded yes with that silly grin plastered on my face.

The next day, Dave called and we made arrangements for our dinner together. After he called, I immediately called my friend Tracy and said, "What the hell am I doing?" before she could even say hello.

Laughing, as I had previously filled her in on all the details, she said, "You're going to have a good time. Just enjoy it. He said 'just friends'."

"I know, but I said I wouldn't date for a while, and here I am going out and I'm way more excited than I should be." And it was true. I was super excited. I felt like I was on the precipice of something big. My adrenaline was pumping, and it felt like time was dragging and speeding by all at the same time.

"Do I get him a birthday card or something?" I asked her the question I had been pondering ever since we made the dinner plans. I mean, it was his birthday after all, but then I didn't really know him. What was the expectation? What was appropriate?

"If you want to, get him one. If not, don't. Otherwise, just be you and have fun. Nothing more than that. Now go decide what you're going to wear." Tracy demanded as we disconnected the call.

The next evening I was wearing my little black and denim sundress with black strappy sandals. It was casual, because I wanted to remind myself to keep it casual, but it was also the first time he'd be seeing me in a dress. I did have nice legs and wanted to show them off a bit. The doorbell rang and I went to answer it, trying to keep my kids back from the door at the same time.

They were curious to see the "new guy," as they put it. I was doing my best to keep the kids from meeting him until I got to know him better. I was conscious of them getting attached to someone who would not be in the picture for long. As I cracked open the door, planning to slide out and keep the kids behind it, Dave did something I had never experienced on a date before. He presented me with a bouquet of flowers.

Flowers! He brought me flowers for our date when it was his birthday. Wow! I was flattered, honored, and amazed with just a bit of guilt thrown in that I had not gotten him a card after all.

I decided then and there that since he was treating me like a cherished woman, I wanted it to continue. He opened my car door for me and I slid into his truck. When we arrived at the restaurant, I stayed in my seat when he exited the car. I figured if I wanted the cherishing treatment to continue, I needed to set the stage from the start.

After just a moment's hesitation he came around and opened my door, giving me his hand to help me from the truck. I smiled gratefully and we made our way into the restaurant.

The time passed quickly as we discovered more and more of what we shared in common. We held much of the same beliefs. We were both spiritual but not religious. We liked many of the same things, and then I found out he was reading a book that my psychic had just told me I needed to read.

It was like a lightning rod to my heart and head at the same time. Bam! I knew in my gut that I was supposed to be with this man. It was way too soon and way too fast, but I was ready to just let it unfold.

I knew I had to apply what I learned from John Gray. I could not control the relationship, but I could control my actions and myself. I could let him lead and hunt. I could take my time and really get to know this man. It did not all have to happen wham, bang! Look where that had led me before. No, thank you. I would make sure I was not always available. I would keep my life filled with my other enjoyments as well as make room for him. I would not give up who I was to please him. I would be transparently me, and if that was not what he wanted, I was OK letting him move on. I was determined to enjoy the journey we were starting, to embark upon while it lasted. And one of the most important things I reminded myself was that if I felt that I needed to "fix" any part of him, then I shouldn't be with him. Either he was inside my values and boundaries or he wasn't. No more blurring those lines. No more accepting things that weren't OK with me and just hoping I could change them or they'd get better on their own.

Dave didn't kiss me at the end of the date, nor on the next several, as we were trying to maintain just being friends. I felt he wanted to kiss me as much as I wanted to kiss him, and a part of me wanted to initiate it. This kept the inner dialogue in my head going at a frantic pace as I tried to remember what I had learned from John Gray and keep it in place. Let him do the initiating and chasing. Period.

Letting go of control was the scariest thing for someone like me who'd tried so desperately to stay in control, yet it was also the most liberating, stress-reducing, happiness-creating thing I could do. It sounded so simple, and yet I made it into a big, impossible to do thing.

As I continued my inner journey of letting go and enjoying the moment, surprising things began to happen. We were at our favorite dancing place when Dave asked me to walk out to his truck with him. He said he had something for me. "Of course!" I happily replied.

He reached down and took my hand in his. That instantly brought a smile to my face and excitement beating in my heart. Imagine that—just holding hands brought me bliss. The feel of his large, callused hand wrapped securely around my soft, small hand made me feel loved, safe, and taken care of—all of that in a touch. It was amazing, and I enjoyed savoring those feelings as we walked to his truck.

As I stood to the side waiting for him to retrieve whatever he had brought for me, he reached into his truck and brought out a beautiful red rose. My eyes lit up as I reached for it and took a deep breath, drawing in the sweet scent.

"It came from my garden, and it made me think of you," Dave said, drawing closer to me. As I opened my mouth to reply, he leaned down and kissed me. The kiss began as tender and hesitant and then turned into a deep and passionate one as our tongues danced the ancient dance of love. My knees felt weak and as if they would give out on me at any moment while the desire swirled through my senses. In that moment I felt my heart fall the rest of the way into love and my soul open fully to its partner.

It was a slow courtship, but that was the beginning. We took our time. We got to really know each other—the good, the bad, and the ugly. We knew we were in love. We knew we didn't want to be with anyone else. We also knew that we needed to be sure that neither of us was repeating past patterns.

Dave and I dated for four years before he proposed, even though he often introduced me as his future wife. When he would do that my response was always "You can't say that. You haven't asked yet." Dave would smile and change the topic.

Because of this, perhaps in part, many people tried to tell me that we would never be married, that he was just stringing me along, that he was just not that into me. In my gut I knew that there was something different here. Something that wasn't obvious to everyone else. This time I listened to myself.

The few times we did discuss the possibility of marriage, I told him what I wanted. I wanted a real proposal. I wanted the bended knee, the romantic night, the ring picked by him. I had never had that before, and I finally believed I deserved that fairytale.

On the night of our four-year anniversary, I got my fairytale. Dave had taken me to dinner at the same restaurant where we'd had our first date. We were talking while we were waiting for our meal, and he stood up. I assumed he was going to the restroom, when all of a sudden he dropped to one knee in front of me.

At that moment the rest of the room faded away. In my perfect little bubble it was just Dave and me. He pulled a ring from his pocket that I couldn't see clearly from the happy tears blurring my vision. He asked me to marry him, and I happily said yes. He slid the ring on my finger and kissed me the way he did that first time.

As he took his seat, the noise from the other diners applauding came crashing back in. Wow! I was engaged. I had the fairytale in front of dozens of witnesses. I could have floated to the ceiling.

It would be another four years before we were married in our own backyard, and we are still together and living in our happily-ever-after. At last I had my sweet revenge. I was happy with myself, my life, my family, and my love. I know the secret to revenge. The absolute best revenge in the world is to be happy—and if you're truly happy, revenge no longer matters.

CHAPTER 10

CODEPENDENT MAMA

I had at last found my happily-ever-after and ridden off into the sunset with my Prince Charming, who was disguised as a cowboy. So wasn't that the end of the story? Everything is perfect from now on, right? I mean, that's where all the good romance movies end.

Instead, that nasty old codependence thing would once again rear its ugly head in my world. I thought I'd licked it because my love life was finally on track. Wrong! What I hadn't realized is that it had crept into my parenting as well, and it showed up the most with my youngest child, Adam.

Holding down a demanding full-time job, raising three kids on my own, and trying to maintain healthy relationships with my family, friends, and Dave took just about every ounce of energy I had. While I had gotten pretty good at holding my boundaries with everyone else, at home they still seemed to get blurry.

The kids had rules to follow and chores to do, and I made every effort to let them know they were loved. Looking back I could see how I let those boundaries blur. Of course, hindsight is 20/20. While I was living it I couldn't understand what was missing and mostly just chalked it up to there being no father figure in their lives.

The truth was that the boundaries were not solid, and therefore, untrustworthy. One of the kids would break a rule and I would tell him he was grounded or take away an item she enjoyed for two weeks. After three or four days of the "punishment," if he acted good by behaving, no back-talking, and doing his chores, I'd end the grounding early. I repeated that pattern with each child, but it seemed to happen with Adam the most.

I think I responded that way because a part of me felt guilty that the kids had no active father in their lives. Another part of me was just too tired to deal with it. I wanted my kids to be happy. I wanted them to love me, and I wanted close relationships with them. I found myself struggling to not step back into "Victimville" again.

Adam was a whirlwind from the beginning. He was always full of energy and very bright, often too bright for his own good. In elementary school he figured out that by acting up in class they'd call me and I'd have to come get him early from school. He used this to avoid school and spend one-on-one time with me—even though he spent it in trouble.

His penchant for getting into trouble and challenging authority continued to escalate, until by the time he was thirteen years old I knew something drastic had to be done.

I had begun to suspect that Adam was using drugs, and his behavior at home was abhorrent. Every day was a battle. Gone was the delightful child with a wicked sense of humor. In his place was a mean-spirited teenager who threatened to kill me and everyone around him. He constantly told me how much he hated me and what a lousy mother I was.

I had to lock up my purse when I was home or he'd steal from it. I locked my bedroom door when I left for work or he'd destroy my things or take them. Home was no longer a peaceful retreat. It had escalated into a battlefield.

Searching for help for Adam and my family was almost as stressful as the fights going on inside our home. If he wasn't fighting with me, he fought with his brother and sister. Everyone on the outside had advice, and I tried to follow it all, but nothing seemed to work.

I did find a summer program designed for teens who were struggling. It was six weeks long and cost $5,000. I depleted my savings and sent him with high hopes. I was praying for something to turn him around before it was too late. It was obvious to me that nothing else was working.

Those six weeks were like a breath of fresh air in the home. I had no idea how wound up I'd been. The negative energy in the house had been so thick that I swear I could have cut it with a knife. When he left for his summer trip I saged the house just to dispel as much of the heavy, negative energy as possible.

I walked from room to room with the smoking sage stick, wafting its sweet scent as I concentrated on waving it into every nook and cranny. I imagined the smoke capturing the negative energy and carrying it away, and I began to breathe a little deeper and easier. My shoulders dropped down from where they had been lodged full of tension around my ears.

Ah, yes. This is what calm felt like. I'd been caught up in the hurricane of chaos for so long that I'd forgotten what this felt like. It felt good, but it also made me realize just how bad it had really gotten. Sometimes that was hard to see when I was caught up in it. I was determined to keep this peace after Adam came home. I hoped the camp would teach him the behaviors and coping skills he needed to turn his life around, because the way he was going, he was going to end up dead. Either I was going to kill him, or someone else would. That was my way of letting off steam. I didn't really mean it.

When Adam came home, his behavior initially was changed. There were no more threats. He did his chores, and we all seemed to get along better. Then, I began noticing his old pattern of poor behavior start to creep into our day-to-day lives. A small rebellion here, a harsh word there.

I began looking into military schools, as I was determined to not go back to living in constant chaos. I quickly discovered that military schools had changed. They were no longer the place to send a kid with behavioral issues. They were only for kids who were doing well in school and wanted to be there. That certainly left my son out.

I continued digging for other options and found a program specifically designed for kids with behavioral issues. They had several facilities around the United States. None were in California, as we are considered an "at will" state, which basically meant that if the child decided he didn't want to be there, he could leave. The program cost $30,000 a year.

I certainly didn't have $30,000 lying around, and I really couldn't afford it, but I knew I also couldn't afford to let my son continue down his dark path and bring the entire family with him. So I refinanced my house, putting myself further in debt than I ever wanted to be, but knowing it was worth it if it saved his life.

I secretly enrolled him in the program, only telling Dave and my parents and brothers. I thought that if he knew he would bolt and then be truly lost. I devised a plan to get him safely to Montana where the school was waiting for him.

I told him that his Uncle John wanted to take him camping in Montana but that I didn't think he deserved to go. He immediately asked what he could do to change my mind. I told him that I didn't know, but that I would think about it, and in the meantime his uncle needed to borrow his foot trunk to pack for the trip. He willingly gave me the foot trunk and was on his best behavior while I tried to "decide."

I gave him chores to do to earn the privilege of going while I secretly packed his foot trunk with the items listed on the "To Bring" list from the school.

My younger brother John agreed to come over and pick up the packed trunk, and then at the designated time take Adam to the airport and fly with him to Montana. I had written a letter authorizing John to take him on this trip and to use force if necessary. John was the only person I could trust to do this, and he was big enough to carry it off. My little brother was six foot three and full of muscle, and I knew he had the strength to handle it if Adam figured out what was going on and rebelled at the airport. I didn't want my brother in trouble for helping me out. I also included a letter to be given to Adam after his arrival at the school. In that letter I explained that I had lied about this trip and why he was where he was.

Fortunately for everyone involved, Adam was so excited to be going on a camping trip out of state with his uncle, whom he greatly admired, that he never caught on to the deception until he arrived at the school. John called me after he left Adam at the school to let me know how it went.

"The plane ride was good. He had no idea what was happening until after we were at the school. When we got there and were sitting in the office, I asked him if he knew what was going on, and he said no." As I listened to John, my heart filled with gratitude that everyone was safe and he hadn't had to fight Adam on the way.

"I told him where he was and why, gave him your letter, and then they checked him in."

"What was his response?"

I heard a catch in John's voice as he told me, "Tell my mom I love her and that I understand."

My heart squeezed at those words and then eased, as it affirmed for me that I had done the right thing. No matter what anyone else said. No matter that people couldn't understand or comprehend what I had done to save my family. For us, it was the right thing. Those words I hung onto like a life raft for the next three years that Adam took us on a wild ride in the program.

The program could be completed in a year, but kids all went through it at different paces. Parents could also pull their kids from the program. I chose to make a promise to myself and Adam that he would be in the program until he completed it or turned eighteen and left on his own.

The kids completed the program by earning privileges, participating in and completing seminars, and demonstrating good choice abilities. There were seminars for the parents and family members to attend as well and ones the parents and kids did together.

I sent Adam to the program to get "fixed." I didn't understand where I had gone wrong with him. Ben and Leyna appeared to be fine, but Adam was off the deep end. What had happened? I couldn't figure out why everything was so different with him.

It was such a slippery slope that I was dancing on. It was easy to hear that old familiar inner critic as I blamed myself for everything wrong in my family. That critic was reinforced as I saw the judgment in people's eyes when they learned that I had sent my son out of state into a program that used what could be construed as extreme methods to straighten him out.

Ben's girlfriend even told me that she believed I was making a mistake and that I should send Adam to her grandmother in Mexico instead. She believed that her family could set him straight.

All I heard in my mind was that everyone thought I was a bad mother and that I was continuing to make poor choices. Evidence of what a bad person I was played out like a video in my head. Look at all I had been through. Look at how many times I was victimized. I seemed to invite bad into my life.

Then a quiet voice whispered a reminder of the words Adam said when he realized he was being enrolled into the program, "Tell my mom I love her and I understand."

If my son could intuitively understand that this was necessary, then I could, too. I would go to every seminar offered and learn everything I could to improve my family's life. I even sent Ben, his girlfriend, and Dave to every one of the seminars they could attend. I wanted my family on the same page, and I figured that if we were all learning the same tools, our communication could only improve.

After one seminar about values and boundaries, I had another awakening. I realized that in my need to be needed and loved by my children, I had let those home boundaries blur. I didn't trust myself to be a good mother, and so I wasn't. I wasn't a bad mother, either; I was just a struggling one. I could recognize it for what it was now—codependency. I had been trying to fix everything for my kids instead of allowing them to learn for themselves and trusting them to handle their own lives and decisions while providing guidance instead of control.

The unintentional message I was sending to them was that I didn't believe they could make their own choices, and that I didn't believe in them, period. I knew I had given them the tools to know the difference between right and wrong and that I was always going to be there as a support person to them. Now I needed to allow them to use those skills.

I came home from that seminar and called a family meeting with Dave, Ben, and Leyna. I was accountable for not being clear on our home values and holding steady boundaries. A new chapter was beginning. I declared that it would be different going forward.

Together we defined our family values, and I distinctly spelled out the boundaries and rules for our home. I also spelled out the consequences for each time someone stepped outside a value.

Ben was the first to test the boundaries and consequences. He was nineteen and once again living with me while he saved money until he could find his own place. I didn't expect him to get my permission to go places or stay out, but I did expect him to let me know when he would be home so that I wouldn't worry. Prior to this last seminar, he would often go out and tell me he would be home at 1:00 and then not show up until 7:00. By then I would be worried that something had happened to him and wanting to call his phone, his friends, and the hospitals. I told him several times how disrespectful I found this, and he always swore he would change that pattern.

The new consequence for stepping outside of this boundary was that he would be given an immediate thirty-day notice to move out. I considered respect an important value in my home. It wouldn't matter whether he was financially ready or not. Now I had to be ready to enforce it and live with it.

One week after our family conference, where everything was discussed and agreed upon, Ben slipped right into his old pattern. My heart ached as I stressed over asking my son to leave, knowing that he didn't have the finances in place. Yet I knew that if I gave him a second chance, like I was tempted to, nothing would change in our home, and Adam would be coming home to the same old patterns of second, third, and fourth chances, making it easy for him to slip back into chaos.

"Ben, we need to talk." I said, gathering my inner strength and steeling myself to hold steady and firm.

"Sure, Mom," he said with a smile and sat at our country-style kitchen table with green trim.

I gave him a half-smile back and watched his smile falter. His now panicked expression told me he knew it was serious. I figured the best way through this was to be direct and do my best to keep my emotion out of it.

"We have a broken agreement, Ben."

He hung his head while shrugging his shoulders and said, "Oh. That."

"Do you acknowledge you broke the agreement?"

"Yeah, I guess I did."

"OK. What did I say the consequences would be if that happened again?"

"That I have thirty days to move out." His faced paled, and I saw his Adam's apple bob as he swallowed.

"Right. This is your thirty-day notice, son. I know you'll figure out what to do. I love you." I was proud of myself for staying calm and not breaking into tears. I left him sitting there, the possibilities of what he could do zooming through his head.

Twenty-five days later he moved into an apartment. Three months after that he thanked me for holding that boundary. He acknowledged that he probably wouldn't have moved out for a long time or learned that he could be resourceful if I hadn't done that.

Adam was kept informed of the happenings at home through letters and phone calls. When he heard that his brother had moved out due to a broken agreement, something shifted in him. I think he began to believe that things were really different at home.

When he finally graduated the program and came home at sixteen, it was to a peaceful home centered on values and boundaries. We began to learn to live together again and get to know the people we had become while apart.

As the year progressed Adam picked, pushed, and pulled at every boundary I had. He was still a teenager, after all. What changed was my response. I had learned that his lashing out at me rarely actually had anything to do with me. Usually it was due to someone else, and I was the safest person to unleash his frustration and anger on. I had also learned that by his causing drama, he could deflect or ignore what was really going on inside of himself.

My job was to not get caught up in the drama, but to stay centered, calm, and focused until what was really going on could be uncovered. To do this I became "Mom zombie." No matter what he said or did, I would continue what I was doing, such as reading a book or watching TV. I would tell him in a calm, monotone voice that when he was ready to have an adult conversation about what was really going on with him, I'd be there for him.

I would suggest that he go to his room until he calmed down and was ready for that conversation.

Not getting the normal reaction to his acting out, only getting the "Mom zombie" response, he'd eventually calm down and I would ask questions from a place of curiosity until the truth revealed itself.

Things were better with us, yet I sensed that Adam was struggling. He didn't say much, but I knew from what he told me that making and keeping friends who weren't into partying and defying their parents at every turn was difficult.

As I got ready to go out of town for three days to a work conference, I called Ben to ensure he was coming over to stay at the house with Leyna and Adam while I was gone. I would only be four hours away in Monterey, but I felt that there was too much peer pressure happening to leave Leyna and Adam by themselves. I got the kids off to school and then drove with a coworker to Monterey.

We had checked into our hotel and unpacked and then settled down to eat some lunch before the conference began when my phone rang. It was Adam's school doing a welfare check on him.

My heart pounded so hard in my chest that I thought it would burst through as I listened to the school official tell me that Adam had left school and had been telling his friends goodbye before he did. They said they were concerned, because it didn't sound like just a kid cutting class. It sounded like he was saying goodbye forever.

I tried to stifle the rising panic as I dialed my home and was only getting the answering machine. I began yelling into the machine, uncaring that the other restaurant patrons were now staring at me and listening as I called out Adam's name, demanding he pick up the phone.

I hung up and called back repeatedly until someone picked up the phone. By now, my coworker and I had left the restaurant, and she went to tell my supervisor that we were leaving, and why.

One of Adam's friends finally picked up the phone.

"Adam tried to hang himself, but he's OK. I called 9-1-1 and they're here now."

"What happened? I don't understand. I'm on my way, but I'm four hours away! Let me talk to him. What is going on?" I rattled off questions and demands in rapid fire. I must have frightened the kid, because he handed the phone to the sheriff who had arrived.

I was doing my best to not become hysterical while we clamored into the car and my coworker began driving me home.

"Who is this?" demanded the sheriff in a clipped voice.

"I'm Adam's mother. I'm out of town on a business trip and got a phone call from Adam's school. Please tell me he's OK. I need to know what's going on."

"He's fine. The paramedics are with him. Now, do you know why he's not in school?"

"What?" I asked in stunned disbelief. My son had just tried to hang himself and this doofus was wondering if I knew why he wasn't at school? "He left for school before I left for my trip. His older brother was coming over after school to stay with him and his sister while I was gone. I don't know why he did this. Please, I need to talk to him."

"You need to calm down and talk with me right now. Is it possible that Adam is on drugs?"

Adam's previous history of drug use rolled through my mind as I wanted to scream "No," but I knew I couldn't honestly say it wasn't a possibility. He hadn't been displaying any of the signs, but maybe I missed something. So I replied, "It's possible. He has in the past, but I don't think he is."

"OK, so he's a drug user," the sheriff responded as I heard him scribbling in his notebook.

"No, I didn't say that." I protested, "I said he has in the past."

The sheriff continued to grill me about why I wasn't at home, ensuring that my son stayed in school all day, implying that I was an irresponsible mother because I went out of town on a business trip. If I could have reached through the phone I would have smacked him a good one. How insensitive could someone get?

In the background I could hear Adam starting to have a panic attack. He had been having them off and on over the last several months. I seemed to be the only person who could talk him out of them. His breathing became very labored and he thrashed about.

I told the insensitive jerk of a sheriff to put the phone next to Adam's ear so I could talk him down. Surprisingly, he complied.

Once I had Adam's panic attack stopped, they told me which hospital they were taking him to and disconnected the call. For the rest of the journey, I made phone calls to Dave, Ben, my parents, and my best friend, Holly.

I needed everyone. Ben and my mother went to the hospital to stay with Adam until I could arrive. Dave I needed for support when I got home, because

I was struggling to hold it together. And Holly? I leaned on her for what I considered the hardest task.

I asked her to go to my house and remove all the evidence she could of Adam's suicide attempt. I didn't want Leyna to come home and find that. After that, she stayed with Leyna until we all got home.

I later learned that Adam had propped open our screen security door and left the front door unlocked. He then made one last phone call to a friend and tied his socks around the ceiling fan in the living room. His friend knew something was seriously wrong and raced over to our house with another guy, where they got to Adam just moments after he had stepped off the coffee table, attempting to hang himself. The fact that he had propped open the screen door and left the front door unlocked told me that he really wanted to be rescued; otherwise, if he had locked everything up it was like Fort Knox, no one would have been able to get to him.

They had lifted him up and cut him down before that attempt became successful, and then called 9-1-1. I'll be ever grateful to those two young men. Holly had to finish removing the socks and threw away the suicide note he had written. Then she straightened up the living room and waited for Leyna. There was no one besides Dave and her who I could have asked to do that. I trusted her completely, and she was there for me without hesitation. For that and so many other reasons, she is my sister at heart and I will always love her.

I spent the next few days with Adam going through a psyche evaluation, and the psychologist told me he was the most mature, well-adjusted kid she had ever treated for attempting suicide. This left me feeling even more lost and confused.

Why had he done it? What was so bad that he wanted to permanently get out of life? Things had seemed better at home. What was I missing?

A few months after he had been released and still seemed to be struggling, I made him an offer.

"You seem to be having a hard time. I want to support you. I want to help you, but I don't know how. If you think going back to the program for six weeks will help you get your head straight, I'm willing to do that for you. I will figure out the money somehow. That's not your worry. I just want you to get better."

After spending three years in the program, it was a place of comfort for Adam. He knew the structure, he knew what to expect, and everyone there was clean and sober. I thought that maybe a break from the outside world would help him decide what he really wanted out of life. Thankfully, I was right, and he took me up on my offer.

"Yes, I think going back would be a good thing for me, but just for a little while. I don't want to go back in for the next two years," he said with a nervous smile.

"Done!" I smiled back and gave him an extra long hug.

When he returned six weeks later, he appeared a changed young man. He acted grounded and centered. He discussed concerns with me. He appeared much happier than I had seen him in years.

What I had learned throughout this trying time was that I needed to be clear and define my values and boundaries in all aspects of my life. I stopped playing the blame game. It didn't matter whose fault anything was. It only mattered whether the choices I made were working or not working. If I didn't like the results I was getting, I needed to make different choices. I learned to be accountable for all my choices—working or not. I learned to love myself as a parent as well as what I already loved about me. And I learned that when I tried to do things for others that they could do themselves—and they hadn't asked for my help—I was doing them a disservice. I was really saying, "You can't do that. I'll do it for you, because I can do it better."

Starting with my children, I have learned to treat each person as whole and complete, holding each of their own answers. I am happy to be a supportive, loving mother, wife, daughter, and friend.

CHAPTER 11

PERPETUATING REVENGE

Holding firm to the belief that the best revenge is to be happy, now I had to figure out how to keep it going. Based on the results I was getting, what I was doing was working, and I wanted to continue to grow in that direction. If I hadn't made those changes within myself, the results with Adam would have been far different than what they were. For that matter, my relationship with Dave probably would have tanked.

My attitude toward what I knew I needed, wanted, and deserved in a loving relationship had become healthier. The place from where I made my decisions in regards to a love relationship had changed. Instead of reacting from that scared, unloved little girl place, I now responded as my wise, confident, loving woman.

I now knew that the old self-defeating pattern of a perpetual broken heart was at long last broken. It was time to make that permanent symbol I had tattooed on my body disappear. That heart on the inside of my left ankle with the bolt of lightning and three drops of blood seemed to have the ability to easily yank me back into "Victimville," where I thought I wasn't good enough, pretty enough, smart enough—just plain not enough.

Dave and I had taken a trip to Maui before all the craziness with Adam, and when talking to some of the locals about dolphins, we discovered that they mate for life. When we heard this, Dave immediately took us to the jewelry shop where he purchased a charm for my necklace that had two dolphins facing each other. This was the picture that needed to replace that old broken heart; a symbol of always being together, healing, peace, love, and happiness.

After we returned home from Maui, I snuck off to the tattoo parlor and explained what I wanted to the artist. She drew it up and applied it to the inside of my left ankle, effectively making that symbol that was no longer true for me disappear. Instead I have two dolphins facing each other with the ocean in the shape of a heart in between them. To this day I smile every time I see it, as it reminds me that I give and receive unconditional love constantly.

This does not mean that I don't experience ups and downs in my life. Experiencing just one thing all the time would be like being forced to listen to a monotone speaker for hours on end. Some days are naturally better than others, and I really don't believe that you can be truly happy and positive one hundred percent of the time. The trick is learning to be OK with that, to not numb yourself out when you're not happy and things aren't going your way. Life is a balancing act on a rollercoaster, and it's how you respond to it that makes the difference.

Personally, I love roller coasters—the bigger, faster, and crazier the better. From the first time my dad snuck me on one at the theme park, which I was technically too short to ride, I was hooked. To this day I ride them with my eyes open wide, my hands in the air, and whooping, laughing and screaming, "whoooo hoooo!"

But for the longest time, I didn't apply that to my life when it was going downhill, making a crazy unexpected turn, or even turning upside down. Instead, I took that as my cue to critique my every move while curling into the fetal position and sliding into a funk. I could wallow in that state for days.

Being a codependent, highly sensitive and intuitive person, it was very easy to get caught up in everyone else's stuff. With the tools I've learned throughout all of my experiences, I now have the skills to ride life the same way I rode those rollercoasters—without taking on baggage that doesn't belong to me. That means not taking on other people's stuff. I have learned to be supportive instead of a rescue ranger.

I believe it's important to feel whatever I'm feeling. I mean, really feel it—get down and dirty with it—and then let it go. No more wallowing. Let's face it. The times I gained the most knowledge, wisdom, and experience was when the chips were down and life seemed to suck.

Knowing this makes it much easier for me to deal with whatever is going on. I can experience any event in my life knowing that it's just that—an event.

I had finally learned that the event itself doesn't define who I am; my response does. All events in my life are learning opportunities, and it's up to me to get the most out of it that I can. I now know to root into the depths and relish the highs.

When I numb out, I miss out—not just on the negative, but the positive as well. Every emotion serves a purpose, and I do get that at times some of them can be overwhelming, and most people tend to go into "numb-out mode" just to survive. While this does serve an important purpose, the problem is for those who are living in "Victimville" who only move a short distance and then get stuck in "Survivorhood."

"Survivorhood" over "Victimville" was an improvement in my living situation; however, it's still not an ideal place to live. It's only meant to be a transition place, a temporary stop on my way to "Thrive Town."

In "Victimville" everything "happens to me." My inner critic rules my mind and is constantly proven right by all the bad things that go on. Happiness is fleeting snippets quickly squashed as I'm re-victimized time and time again. No matter what I do, I'll never do enough. I'll try to put up a brave face, but I've truly lost hope that my life will ever be any different.

In "Survivorhood," I'm numbed out to big emotions. I feel the need to fight for what I have and for those other victims that are not ready to stand for themselves yet; thus, I'm in a constant battle mode. I do everything I can to ensure that persecutors are justly punished. I make it day by day and proudly proclaim my survivorship status. I feel better about myself, but I'm still angry and hurt about what happened to me. I haven't quite forgiven the perpetrator, let alone myself. I'm on a constant lookout for the next bully, the next person trying to do me or others harm. Happiness does appear in my world, but it's overshadowed by the pain I hold close to my vest.

In "Thrive Town," I'm fully enjoying the rollercoaster of life. Even in the dark, deep dips, there's an underlying spot of light knowing that whatever I'm experiencing is serving a purpose and bringing a valuable learning opportunity into my life. I've forgiven all those who hurt me, persecuted me, neglected, and abandoned me, including myself. I'm grounded firmly in who I am and what I bring to this life. I know my values and boundaries, and I stand solid within them. I'm supportive to others without feeling the need to rescue or fix them. I challenge myself and others to constantly grow and enrich their lives. I take care of myself and others, knowing that the secret to being balanced is to do both. I live a happy, positive life, being satisfied and grateful for what I have while still reaching to achieve even more.

Having lived in all three places, and knowing that "Thrive Town" is where I want to stay, I also want to increase the population there. The bigger "Thrive Town" gets, the better this planet becomes.

As I write this I can practically hear someone saying, "Yes! I do want to live in "Thrive Town," as it sounds so wonderful, but that's not reality! Bad things still happen in everyone's lives, and I can't live with blinders on, so how can I stay living there?"

The best way I know is to show you with another experience from my life.

I had barely gotten in the door from a long hard day at work when the phone rang. I looked at the caller I.D. and saw that it was my mother. I wondered why she was calling at this time of day, as it was unusual for her. Heaving a deep sigh and rolling my eyes at the interruption to my routine, I picked up the phone to hear her blurt out, "Your dad's had a stroke."

"What? What do you mean?" I squeaked out in a high-pitched tone, stunned and feeling numbness spread over my body while I fought the rising panic, trying to avoid frightening Leyna and Adam, who suddenly had their eyes riveted on me.

"He's had a stroke and I called 9-1-1. They're loading him into the ambulance now." Her voice was firm and sounded calm on the surface, but I could hear the panic and fear rolling underneath. "Where are they taking him, and what do you need from me?" It felt weird asking what she needed from me instead of just saying that I would be right there. One of the things I had learned was that for me to stay in the supporter role instead of moving into the rescuer role, I needed to ask what the person needed. If they needed something, I would then act on that if it was something I could do. It was possible that she would feel better supported if I called people for her or if she needed someone picked up for a ride to the hospital. If I really wanted to be supportive, I couldn't assume what was best for her.

"We're going to Mercy, and I need you there."

"I'm on my way." I hung up the phone and grounded myself, sending the fear, pain and anguish down into the earth and drawing up the energy of love and strength. I would need it to get through this event.

I told Leyna and Adam what happened and that we needed to get to the hospital and then called Ben so he could meet us there.

At the hospital, my mom met us in the lounge and told us what happened. My dad had been outside in hundred-degree weather on a ladder, trimming trees in their backyard. He had an established habit of drinking soda instead of water when he was thirsty, and he followed suit on this day. Later we found out that he had gotten dizzy while on the ladder and fell off of it once, but for then we only knew that he had finished his work and had come in to take a shower before going to a meeting he'd scheduled. My mom realized after a while that he had not come back downstairs, and she went up to check on him. She found him sitting on the toilet, hitting the toilet paper roll over and over. He didn't respond to her. Knowing something was dreadfully wrong, she immediately called 9-1-1.

It ended up that my dad had a massive stroke, partially brought on by heat stroke. His left side was paralyzed, which, given that he was left-handed, affected his recovery even more. He would have to relearn how to eat, write, and live as a right-handed person if he survived.

I had always viewed my dad as the glue of our family. He was the peacekeeper, the guidance counselor, and incredibly intelligent. I knew that if I couldn't figure something out, he would have the answer. He was the only person I knew who appeared to be good at everything. He was reliable, respectful, and generous at heart. He loved to help others, and I always admired him. I had long ago forgiven him for not responding the way I wished he would to some of the tragic events in my life. I couldn't picture my life without him in it.

Both of my brothers lived out of state, and I was the only child nearby. I knew this meant that I was the main person on whom my mother needed to rely. While our relationship was definitely improved since I began to define and hold my boundaries, I still would not have described us as close. A part of me was fascinated that I was her first phone call after 9-1-1 and wondered at the instinctual trust that had arisen in her time of need.

Mom had always been self-sufficient, and operated in her protective shell. She could be fiercely loyal, and had always been solid in her faith. She'd never been a physically demonstrative person, but people always knew if she liked them, or not. Keeping up appearances had always seemed important to her, and I know she was raised to keep her private life private, and to speak up for those who couldn't speak for themselves. I've always believed that she was relied upon heavily as the oldest daughter in her family, and thus she quickly learned to be a caretaker for everyone. That pattern carries on in her life today. She loves to take care of others. She's a woman who's not afraid to voice her opinion and continually strives to do the right thing. My dad was her vulnerable spot, and in the fear of losing him she appeared lost.

I had learned to love my mother for who she was as a human being. Then I came to understand that she loved me and raised me the best she could. Now it was time for me to be there for her. It was what I wanted to do and what I knew my dad would want me to do.

That evening, as I sat with my dad for a bit, holding his hand and talking to him, he suddenly grimaced in pain and squeezed my hand. "Am I going to die?" he asked me with fear in his eyes.

My heart thudded painfully in my chest as I wanted to scream "No!" Yet I wouldn't lie to my dad. I did what I knew he would do; I told the truth. "I don't know, Dad. I do know that I love you and you love me, and that's all that matters."

Tears swam in both of our eyes as we contemplated the possibilities. I don't believe death is a bad thing. I believe it is a natural part of our cycle here on earth. I believe the soul that passes over to the "other side" or "heaven," or whatever you wish to call it, is in a place of peace and love. I also believe that we all still have access to them. It's just different than when they are physically here. I think most people fear death because they're afraid of the unknown, and death is definitely fraught with the unknown. Did this mean that my heart did not ache at the possibility of my dad dying? Heck no!

My dad survived that night, and was later transferred to another hospital to begin the recovery process. The next several months consisted of visiting my dad, consulting with the doctors, ensuring my mom took care of herself, and trying to live as normal a life as possible.

During that time, I held down my full-time corporate job, managed my side business coaching clients to empower themselves and manifest their dreams, spent time with my husband, kids and friends, and continued writing my first book, *Achieving the Balance Dream—11 Secrets to Living A Life of Balance*. When my dad had to go in for emergency brain surgery due to his brain swelling, I took my laptop to the hospital and wrote there.

Did doing these things mean I was insensitive to what was going on? Did I have blinders on to the seriousness of it all? No. I knew that wallowing in self-pity and falling back into "Victimville" would not serve anybody—least of all my dad. I needed to take care of me so that I could take better care of my mom and dad on this journey. If I was burnt out or stuck in the sorrow, I wouldn't be able to be there for anyone. That's what enabled me to be there, however, whenever, and wherever my parents needed me to be.

I dedicated that book to him and was able to share it with him after it was published. I will always cherish the happy tears in his eyes as he listened with pride when I read him the dedication as he sat outside in his wheelchair, visiting with my mom and me. I could have missed out on that if I had just dropped my life and lived in the chaos of what was happening. Instead, I have no regrets.

After another emergency brain surgery, Dad was sent to a hospital in Vallejo to recover. This hospital was supposed to be the best for stroke recovery, and we were hopeful that he would make enough of a recovery to start living at home again. Instead, due to incompetence in cleaning his wound, he ended up with a staph infection in his brain. This severely impacted his recovery to the point that we had no choice but to put him into an assisted living facility. He now needed round-the-clock care due to dementia adding to his struggles. There was no possible way my mother could care for him on her own.

He ended up in and out of so many facilities and hospitals that I lost track. It seemed that no one was equipped to handle a stroke patient with dementia in a wheelchair, paralyzed on the left side and with a missing section of his skull cap they had to remove part of and throw away due to the infection, and whose family was actively involved. It seemed a lot of places didn't like having the family there every day and being active in his care. I always found it strange and disheartening that they would encourage families to stay away in this manner.

As the journey went on, my mom and I had many conversations about when to let go, funeral wishes, life-saving measures, and the like. I seemed to be the only person willing to listen and have an open conversation, looking at all points of view regarding the topic of death.

After eighteen months of this crazy-go-round, my dad chose to pass over to the other side. I was alone with him in his room as it happened. We all knew that his time was close and wanted to show our love to him by being there to say goodbye. Throughout the day we took turns sitting vigil. After many hours of waiting, my older brother had taken a break outside on the balcony with his wife, and my younger brother had gone to pick his wife up from the airport. My mom had left the room to fetch a nurse, and I sat at my dad's side, holding his hand. I remember thinking I needed to go home and get some rest, and being torn between staying and leaving.

I heard in my head, "It's time to go," and thought it meant that I should go home now, so I leaned over and kissed his cheek and whispered in his ear, "I love you, Dad." At that moment he took in one breath and then stopped. I felt love flow through my body and I lifted my eyes toward the sky, feeling his spirit soar up. I whispered "Thank you" to the Divine for letting him go. I felt at peace, I felt joy, and I felt sadness that I would not physically be able to hug him again, all bundled up together.

Several minutes later, my mom walked into the room. I shook my head at her to let her know that he was gone. She rushed to his side, calling his name. I felt as if a piece of him slid back into his wasted body, and then he took a small breath. After a few breaths with long stretches in between, my mom told him she loved him and that it was OK to let go now. His body once again ceased to breathe, and I knew when the remaining part of his soul spirited away.

There was beauty in those final moments, and I will be forever grateful that I had them. Going forward, I knew my relationship with my mom had changed once again. We grew closer in our shared experience, and I like to believe that she now knows that no matter what our differences are, I love her. I am here for her, no matter what.

Through time, forgiveness, personal growth, and understanding, I have come to know that no matter what life hands me, I have the power to choose my responses and aim for win-win results. I am grateful for every learning opportunity given me and I relish my times of joy. And to think where I am today all started the day I decided I wanted revenge. What I discovered was that the absolute best revenge is to be happy—and if I'm truly happy, revenge no longer matters.

How to Turn a Hot Mess into a Happy Success

I want you to find your true happiness, my dear reader, and this is why I needed to be completely transparent in sharing this story with you. I want to provide guidance so that hopefully you can move yourself out of "Victimville" much sooner than Rebecca did—no matter what you've experienced in your life. It's time to stop being victimized and just surviving day-to-day and start thriving in your happily-ever-after. The rest of the chapters in this book are designed to help you do just that, so keep reading to turn your own hot mess into a happy success!

CHAPTER 12

THE CODEPENDENT'S CODE

Codependent people have a code—it's all about others. While that sounds wonderful and generous, it's actually dangerous. They're leaving out an important ingredient in that formula—themselves. If you only take care of others and leave yourself out, eventually you burn out and then you have nothing left to give those who have now come to rely on you. It's important to be all inclusive; take care of yourself and others.

Codependency has been described as a disease. It can certainly feel like one. I felt like an alcoholic, except love was my alcohol. Often people are prescribed the "twelve-step" program to try to gain some control of their codependency.

I had faithfully followed the twelve-step program, yet somehow it took another "Aha moment" as I shared with you in Chapter 1, to begin to create something different in my life. How had I fallen so far "off the wagon" without realizing it? Why didn't it work? Would I have to live out this cycle forever? Could I even have a healthy relationship? What would that look like?

Here is what I have learned about codependency and how to identify if you are codependent.

Codependency is not a disease. It is a learned emotional and behavioral condition which affects the ability to have a healthy relationship with others. The good news is that you can change your condition, choose your behavior, and feel your emotions without letting them run your life.

Recovering from codependency takes time, effort and courage, but in the end, you will feel a greater sense of fulfillment, happiness, playfulness, and peace. A full recovery is possible! You do not have to forever be a "recovering codependent."

A part of being codependent is resistance to playing and having fun. Imagine how joyful your life will be when you have the freedom to give yourself permission to play. When was the last time you let your inner child out to finger paint, play in the dirt, or roll down a hill?

Understanding how you became codependent in the first place is crucial to your healing. As a child you learned a set of behaviors and methods of solving problems that helped you survive an environment of emotional pain and stress. The stress could have come from living with someone with a chemical dependency; physical, sexual or emotional abuse; chronic illness, either mental or physical; or being in a non-loving or hyper-critical environment.

As an adult, a codependent person has little to no sense of self. If you were to look back on your life, you might see that your whole life has been spent in extreme acts to meet others' expectations. Your emotions and thoughts about yourself are based on people's responses to you. For example, if you're nice to me, I'm a good person. If you disagree with me or snap at me, I'm a bad person.

You probably have trust issues, as you've learned not to trust other people or yourself. Someone always gets let down. You seek fulfillment in pleasing other people, but that never really works—because you don't feel you deserve the gratitude or compliments you may receive. It may feel like it's never enough, like you're never enough.

Some of the behaviors you adopted to help you survive may now have become compulsive, which means you do them against your will; you have no control over them. You may not even realize you are doing them. Those behaviors and problem-solving methods are now keeping you from living a life where you feel safe, secure, loved, and fulfilled. Because of them, you keep repeating the same patterns over and over, sometimes with different partners, and you still aren't happy.

Giving and being kind, considerate, empathic, and of service is great, and something the world definitely needs. It turns into codependency when the driving need you have is to please others in order to feel whole as a person. A symptom of low self-esteem is when you think it's not right to take care of yourself or to be assertive. Finding your identity in being a rescuer or martyr is not healthy.

How to recognize if you're codependent:

1. *Do you find yourself constantly needing to "fix" and rescue people?*

    If you're codependent, you are more aware of others' needs and feelings than you are your own. When asked what you want or need, the answer is most often "I don't know." You have a hard time receiving.

2. *Do you easily get caught up in drama?*

    Codependents often get sucked into the drama of others' lives and are so busy rescuing others and sacrificing themselves, they miss what the root of the issues are. They don't have time to deal with their own issues because they're so busy taking care of everyone else. This is really a self-defeating behavior.

3. *Are you trying to control or feel controlled by someone else?*

    Do you need the person more than you love them? Neediness is a hallmark of a codependent relationship. One person's happiness depends completely on the other. They don't know how to make themselves happy. In a true loving partnership, you love each other more than you need each other. Relationships should enhance you, not complete you. You are already whole and complete.

4. *Do you do more than your share?*

    What's the difference between a hard worker and a workaholic? Are you working to live or living to work? Codependents often take their work home with them, answer work calls and emails, no matter if it's after quitting time or they are on vacation. They do not have clearly defined boundaries in their work or relationships.

5. *Are you always seeking approval and recognition?*

    Codependents live their life through their self-limiting beliefs. They believe they are not good enough, dumb, stupid, worthless, and defective. This is their core wound, or sacred wound. It's what drives their choices and decisions and affects what they see when they look in the mirror, and it affects how they talk to themselves. What they don't realize is we all have a sacred wound, but we can choose to rewire where our choices and decisions come from. We can choose to live from our purpose rather than our wounds.

As adults, codependent people seek recognition and approval, but when they get it they are embarrassed. They have difficulty asking others to meet their needs. They don't believe they are worthwhile or lovable. Codependents do not have a strong sense of self. When asked to describe themselves, codependents will give their job title or say "I'm a wife, partner, daughter, and mother."

A non-codependent person will say, "I'm an independent, powerful, compassionate person who enjoys having fun and adventures." There's nothing wrong with being proud of your job or relationships, but those should not be your main identity. Those are things you do, not who you are.

6. *Do you find that you do anything to hold onto a relationship? Do you fear being alone?*

Because codependents have their whole identities tied up in their work and relationships, they have no relationship with themselves. They don't know how to be alone and enjoy that time. They often feel abandoned and unwanted. They don't feel able to express their own feelings or express a difference in opinion for fear of driving the relationship away. They often stay in abusive relationships because they feel nobody else will want them and that's all they deserve.

But there is help. The problem isn't them. It's your relationship with you. Letting go of the need to help can liberate you. Instead of saying "Yes!" to everything and everyone, ending up overwhelmed and exhausted, you have an alternative. You can learn to only say "yes" to things that feed your soul, align with your purpose, and easily fit into your schedule. You can say "No, thank you" without ruining relationships. People do appreciate help, but most really don't want you to do it at the expense of yourself. Plus, when you've overcommitted, you don't have the ability to fully focus and give your best at anything. You are actually doing a disservice to others by not taking care of yourself.

If you are codependent, you can recognize the compulsive behaviors that keep you locked in the repetitive patterns you used as a child. You can learn how to be assertive, how to take responsibility for your own actions, and how to release the fear.

You can learn how to say "No." You can learn to listen and communicate. You can learn it is OK to have needs and to have them fulfilled. Often professional counseling, therapy, or coaching can be helpful to create new, healthy patterns for yourself.

The "problem" is not them. The problem is your belief that this is your proper role and that you are powerless to change it. You may be addicted to caretaking or controlling. If you're codependent, it's a known pattern in your life. We tend to be more comfortable with the known—even if it's unhealthy for us—than stepping into the unknown.

You have to learn how to let go of the need to try to control the people, places, and events in your life. It's this letting go that will provide you the ultimate freedom from shame, fear, and your self-defeating patterns. After all, the only person you can truly control is yourself.

Like any problem, you need to understand what's at the root. You can start from a neutral place. Step outside of your emotions and look at the history of your behavior. Notice the patterns. Determine if the pattern is working for you and how you want your life to be, or if it's holding you back.

When you can get past the emotions and examine facts, write them down. Do a little timeline or a scorecard of non-working behavior. This will help you to focus on the changes you want to make. It can also help you recognize the patterns easier when they crop up again.

Have you identified yourself as a codependent person? Awareness is the first step but can often beg the question, "So now what?" Taking the necessary action to shift from being a codependent person to being a happy, healthy person living life, instead of surviving, can appear overwhelming.

OK, you've got the awareness part down, right? You now notice whenever that codependent tendency pops up in your life. No? You've only read the traits and discovered you're codependent? OK, then. The next step is becoming truly aware. The ability to identify the trait is one step; knowing when it's showing up is another. You can't shift it if you're not aware of it.

You've heard that saying, "The definition of insanity is doing the same thing over and over and expecting different results." It's true. If you continue the same pattern, the same behavior, you will end up with the same codependent results.

It's easy to see the pattern when it's in writing and right in front of you. I recommend getting a journal, or breaking out the one probably growing dust bunnies on it, and keeping track for at least a week. Ideally, track your behaviors for a month, but if that is too overwhelming for you, start with a week.

Notice when you are being a "rescue ranger" to others. Do you feel responsible for others' thoughts, feelings and actions? Feel compelled to "fix" the other person's problem for them? Give unsolicited advice, fix problems without being asked, or take control of others' situations? Only feel good when needed by someone or handling a crisis? When you find yourself in these situations, take note. Journal it. Whether you noted it before, during, or after the situation, put it in your journal. Don't beat yourself up over it; just notice and journal.

Notice when you are over committing yourself and saying "yes" when you really want to say "no." Journal every time you make a commitment to do something.

Notice how many times you do things for others and how many times you do things just for you. Keep a count in your journal. At the end of the week, or month, depending on what you choose, tally up the results. You will most likely find that the more you are aware of the behaviors, the earlier you catch yourself doing them. This is where your golden opportunity to shift begins. When you notice yourself in a codependent behavior, STOP! Take five. Give yourself a few minutes to choose a different behavior. Journal the event. Capture your new choice and what results it brought you. Track the new results. Are they what you want? How do you feel? After at least one week or month of choosing different behaviors, go back and track for the same period the number of times you're still choosing your old pattern and the results it brings you. Has the number lessened? If so, you're on your way. Take a moment to acknowledge and celebrate this.

If not, re-commit and redo the exercise until you begin to see a change. Beating up on yourself is strictly forbidden!

It is also important that you go through the twelve steps. Understand that it is not the end. It's a beginning. The twelve steps clear the path for you to uncover your authentic self and begin really living, instead of just surviving.

A helpful hint: You're free to insert whichever word that best fits for you in terms of "God," such as Spirit, Universe, God, Goddess, Jesus, Allah, Buddha, or Higher Self. Don't let an imagined religious factor interfere with your growth and healing.

The Twelve Steps

1. Admitted we were powerless over our need to control others—that our lives had become unmanageable.

2. Came to believe that a power greater than ourselves could restore us to sanity.

3. Made a decision to turn our will and our lives over to the care of God as we understood Him/Her.

4. Made a searching and fearless moral inventory of ourselves.

5. Admitted to God, to ourselves, and to another human being the exact nature of our wrongs.

6. Were entirely ready to have God remove all those defects of character.

7. Humbly asked Him/Her to remove our shortcomings.

8. Made a list of all persons we had harmed, and became willing to make amends to them all.

9. Made direct amends to such people wherever possible, except when to do so would injure them or others.

10. Continued to take personal inventory, and when we were wrong, promptly admitted it.

11. Sought through prayer and meditation to improve our conscious contact with God as we understood Him/ Her, praying only for knowledge of His/Her will for us, and the power to carry that out.

12. Having had a spiritual awakening as the result of these steps, we tried to carry this message to codependents and to practice these principles in all our affairs.

As you are going through these steps, you can expedite your full recovery by simultaneously following the rest of the steps in this book. People around you may not understand when you begin to make different choices, but your true friends and those who love you will adjust and support you on this journey.

It is necessary to go through the process, to not avoid it or try to circumvent it. The quickest route to recovery is to go through, instead of trying to short cut, the process. It's OK to feel what you're feeling. The difference is that it will no longer run your life. This is where the transformation really begins to take place.

CHAPTER 13

STOP BEING A RESCUE RANGER

The most common trait of a codependent person is the need to help, fix or "rescue" everyone around us. We are often the first person our friends call when they need help, and we usually don't even wait to be asked. We charge in, offering solutions, taking care of things, and become confused and hurt when the other person does not appear grateful.

Codependents really do want to help. It's their generous hearts that motivate them to try to be everything to everyone but themselves. Instead, as a "Rescue Ranger," they are often seen as controlling. The truth is that inside, they feel out of control, so they focus outward instead and try to control situations and people around them under the guise of helping them. Really, it's a cry for help. I know that inside I wished that someone would step in and take control for me so I no longer had to, while at the same time I didn't trust anyone else to take that control.

One of the most important and critical moves in healing from codependency is to learn how to stop rescuing others and become supportive instead. Here's what I discovered and clung to as my motivation whenever I was tempted to jump in and help.

When I thought I was helping friends, family, and coworkers, or even sometimes a stranger, I was actually hurting them. I was sending them an unconscious message that I didn't believe that they were capable of handling it on their own. I was feeding their negative machine.

I found this out in a painful manner, as I described to you in Chapter 10, with my youngest son, Adam. It took the universe whapping me upside the head with a two-by-four for me to get this lesson. Looking back over my life, I can see where it showed up time and time again. I was just too busy "fixing" everything and everyone to notice. I want to help you avoid the two-by-four and learn it here and now.

I'm not saying never help others. Of course we all could use help from time to time. It's learning when it's appropriate and supportive to help instead of presumptuous and controlling. I'm giving you the tools you need to be able to make that discernment.

When you feel the urge to jump in and rescue someone, STOP! Ask yourself the following questions first.

1. Did they ask for my help?

2. Do they have the tools and resources to fix it themselves?

3. Do I believe they were capable of handling it themselves?

4. Why do I want to help? Because it will make me feel better, smarter, needed?

5. What will happen if I don't help?

If they asked for your help and it is within your abilities to do so, then by all means help, but don't take over. Find out specifically what they need from you, and then give what is within your resources to do.

If they have not asked you for help and they have the tools and resources to fix it themselves, butt out. If you're not sure about the tools and resources, let them know that you have some to share, but only if they wish. Or simply ask them what it is they need from you to best support them.

If you believe they are capable of handling the situation for themselves, let them. The greatest learning comes with our greatest challenges and struggles. You are robbing them of that growth opportunity if you do it for them. The majority of people are whole and complete and capable of amazing strength, if we give them the opportunity to use it. Often, just knowing you believe in them gives them all the support they need.

When I feel the urge to jump in and "fix it," because either it appears that no one else is doing it or I don't believe they're doing it as well as I could, I stop and look at what my motivation is behind helping. Look deep, not just on the surface. If my motivation is purely to help and be supportive, not take control and look for praise, which as a codependent I wouldn't accept anyway, then I offer to help. "Ask before you leap" is a good mantra to help control the urge to leap in and fix without being asked.

When asking yourself what could happen if you didn't help, do so with the understanding that you cannot control how others respond to anything. You can only control your response. If you don't help, will the project fail? If so, what's the worst that could happen? If you don't help, will the person endanger herself or someone else? If you don't help, will the consequences be an opportunity for those involved to learn from the situation?

If you've gone over these questions and come to the decision to help, the healthiest way to do it in a supportive manner is to ask the individual(s), "How can I best support you right now?"

Offering help in this manner does a couple of things; it allows the person to feel in control of the situation, knowing that you don't want to take over. It lets them know you care and want to help in the way they need you to, and it helps hold you within the boundary of being supportive instead of acting codependent.

Sometimes a person may not know what you can do to best support them; that is the time to offer some suggestions of things you could do. It is important, while doing so, to assure them that you believe in them and know that they are capable of doing this themselves, but that you want to help because you love them and wish only to make it easier for them. I also iterate that I do not want to take over, that I just want to help, especially with those relationships in which I have previously acted as codependent. It's a gentle reminder for them and myself that I will no longer take that role.

Learning to be supportive instead of a "Rescue Ranger" takes time and practice. It may feel strange or even wrong sometimes. I implore you to have patience with yourself, at the very least as much patience as you would have with your dearest friend.

The good news is that with awareness, no matter where in the act you catch yourself, you can implement this healthy tool.

Getting completely out of the drama triangle can be a difficult process, as you are retraining yourself to respond differently than you have for probably the majority of your life. Be as compassionate with yourself as you would with someone else who was working to change something within herself.

One of the tools I used to move from "Victimville,"—otherwise known as "the drama triangle" by Karpman—to "Thrive Town" was pinning the diagrams and their correlation in a place where I could easily view it every day. Whenever I was facing a decision, I would study the chart and try to evaluate what role I was in when making my choice.

I've included the diagram and descriptions here for you:

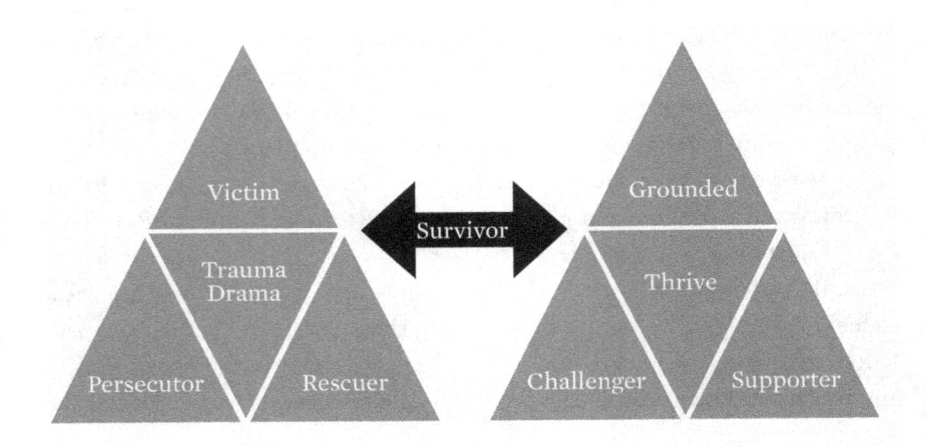

```
        Victim                              Grounded
      Trauma                                  Thrive
      Drama         ⟵ Survivor ⟶
Persecutor    Rescuer              Challenger    Supporter
```

The first triangle is the drama triangle credited to Karpman. The drama triangle has three roles: the **Victim**, the **Rescuer**, and the **Persecutor**. The glue that binds these roles together is lack of personal power and unclear personal values and boundaries. People don't know who they are, or where they end and another person begins. Any perceived boundaries become blurred because the person continuously jumps from one role to another, and so on.

The *Victim* is a person who feels helpless, blames others, and feels sorry for herself: "If it weren't for my boss, I'd be _____ (rich, happy, successful)." By blaming others, the victim surrenders her power, which is what keeps her feeling helpless and powerless.

The *Rescuer* is a person who takes care of everyone else. Oftentimes this is a child of an addictive family who feels it is her responsibility to solve the family's problems and take care of the addict. Within the role of rescuer is the victim consciousness.

These two roles are most often where the codependent person falls or jumps back and forth the most. The victim and rescuer are naturally attracted to one another and thereby perpetuate the codependent relationship with one another. The rescuer is constantly trying to "fix" the victim, which results in the victim feeling even more helpless and eventually even resentful. In turn, this resentment can bring about a role reversal, wherein the victim becomes the persecutor.

The *Persecutor* persecutes the rescuer, and then the rescuer becomes the victim. Persecutors can be physically, emotionally, or sexually abusive; they may persecute by withdrawing love, sex, or money. They usually are very passive-aggressive and use guilt as a way to control and manipulate others. Interestingly enough, then the persecutor feels pity for the victim and moves to the rescuer position. The victim resents feeling helpless and having to be rescued and begins to persecute the rescuer. The triangle takes on a life of its own, and off they go, forever stuck in "Victimville" and unable to find their way out.

The Survivor arrow in between is when you are living in "Survivorhood." Here, you're numbed out to big emotions and you miss out on the joy of living, but you are content with just surviving right now. You feel the need to fight for what you have and for those other victims who are not ready to stand for themselves yet, thus, you are in constant battle mode. You do everything you can to ensure persecutors are justly punished. You make it day by day and proudly proclaim your survivorship status. You feel better about yourself, but you're still angry and hurt about what happened to you. You haven't quite forgiven the perpetrator, let alone yourself. You're on constant lookout for the next bully, the next person trying to do you harm. Happiness does appear in your world, but it's overshadowed by the pain you hold close to your vest. In this state, it's easy to slip back into the drama triangle from time to time.

The thrive triangle is my creation as an answer to how to remain out of the drama triangle and live a happier, healthier life.

The thrive triangle also has three roles: the **Grounded**, the **Supporter**, and the **Challenger**. The glue that binds these roles together is a set of clearly defined values and boundaries that are effectively communicated to all parties. People know that they are whole and complete, and enjoy enhancing each other's lives as well as their own. They make their decisions from their purpose rather than their core wound.

The *Grounded* is a person who is self-aware and stands in their integrity. They are able to evaluate their emotions, feel them, and then let them go. They do not play the blame game. Instead, they look at what is working or not working in their lives. They're unable to be manipulated by guilt or take on other people's baggage. They have forgiven themselves and anyone who has hurt them, and they understand that every event and person who touches their lives is a gift and learning opportunity.

The *Supporter* is a person who is willing and happy to help others, but they don't do so to the detriment of themselves. They are able to say "No" when something is outside their values or they don't have the time or energy to do it. They are compassionate without being sucked into drama. Instead of believing that they know what is best and what everyone needs, they ask, "How can I best support you right now?" and then follow through in meeting those needs. They are able to actively listen to others' wants, desires, and needs, and can play the role of cheerleader or advisor when asked.

The *Challenger* is a person who supports your excellence but not your crap. They ask questions from a place of love and curiosity, pushing you to dream and achieve more than you thought possible. They help you stretch outside your self-imposed limitations. They make a great coach or accountability partner.

The great news with the thrive triangle is that you can move between the roles fluidly based on what your individual situation calls for. Living here keeps you squarely in "Thrive Town," creating your own happiness and supporting others in creating theirs.

CHAPTER 14

YOUR LINE IN THE SAND

You have probably noticed a recurring theme throughout this book—boundaries. So what's the big deal about boundaries? Boundaries are crucial to all relationships, whether they're personal, familial, or in business. The purpose of having boundaries is to protect and take care of ourselves. The majority of people do not intend to hurt or offend us, and we need to be able to effectively communicate what that means to us so they can understand. Every person has the right to protect and defend themselves—not only the right, but the duty to take responsibility for how we allow others to treat us.

We all have perceived boundaries, so having them really isn't the issue—holding them is. Experience has shown me that if you're wobbly in holding your boundaries, you can't trust yourself, and if you can't trust yourself, no one else will trust you either.

Whether we're conscious of it or not, we all want boundaries. Boundaries help us to feel secure, to understand how to best meet ours and others' needs. It is the foundation in building trust. We all instinctively push at boundaries, not because we want to break them, though it often appears that way, but because we want to know that they are firm and solid and that we can trust them.

Trust is a key ingredient in all relationships and in manifesting happiness and success. Think about someone you know who is wobbly in their boundaries. Maybe it's even you. You've seen them let people run amok all over them. Do you fully trust them, or is there something about them that keeps you from completely relying on them for anything?

Remember this when it comes to your own relationships. If you have not clearly defined your boundaries and do not hold them with integrity, the people in your life cannot fully trust you. This will keep tension in your relationships and can get in the way of communication. Your relationship will definitely suffer, as it will not be able to enhance your life the way it could.

Remember what happened in Chapter 8 when I finally defined and held my boundaries with my mom? It completely transformed our relationship. At first, it meant I felt I had to let go of the relationship completely. Sometimes in order to hold that line, you have to be willing to let go of the relationship. If you don't, you've just blurred the boundary line and are back to a lack of trust.

I have found that the majority of the time, whatever or whomever I was willing to let go of came back better than I ever expected.

So how do you decide what your boundaries are? In order to set realistic boundaries that are true for you, you need to know what your values are.

Personal values may come from circumstances and experiences in your life and can change over time. Personal values are implicitly related to choice; they guide decisions by allowing for an individual's choices to be compared to each choice's associated values.

Business values often mirror your personal values and should be set based on your services, products, and expectations of your clients. You need to be clear on what you expect from your clients and what they can expect from you.

I have found that it is helpful to not only define what your values are, but your definition of said values. A lot of people may say that integrity is one of their values, but what does integrity mean to them? How do they know when they or others are acting in integrity? Spell it out. As an example, I'll share my definition of integrity: commitment, self-worth, value of your word.

Write out the values that are important to you and that you expect in your day-to-day life, such as honesty, family, fun, adventure, integrity, and acceptance. You may end up with a list of twenty or more. You want them easy to remember, so once you have that initial list, see which ones can be covered by other ones. For example, can honesty be listed under integrity for you? Try to distill it down to five or six core values. You don't have to; I have thirteen, but it sure is easier to remember.

Now write out the definitions of each core value. Post it somewhere you can see it constantly. I suggest having a personal one posted next to your mirror or on your refrigerator where you can see it daily, and post your business values in your office.

Once you have this, it is much easier for you to set your boundaries. If something is outside your value frame, it's outside your boundary. This is why clarity on definitions is so important. If you said no drugs or alcohol for your value of health, you've just said you won't be taking any aspirin or prescribed medications. Be very clear so you can remain in total integrity with yourself and those you are in a relationship with.

Boundaries are limits or barriers that protect you, your emotions, time, and energy. When your boundaries are well defined, they help to prevent misunderstandings or conflict within your relationships. Setting and holding boundaries is a way of defining who you are and what you stand for. It's our responsibility to take care of and protect ourselves.

Setting boundaries also means being accountable for your choices and the results they net you. You make the choice. You're accountable for that choice and the end result. If you don't like the result, make a new choice. Remember, it's not about playing the blame game; it's about whether it's working for you or not. You can't control other people's behavior, but you can control your response to it.

For example, I don't allow people to make racist remarks around me. Now, I can't control what they will say, but I can control whether I continue to listen. I can let them know that they are crossing my line, and if they continue I will walk away.

To solidly hold your boundaries, you need to be able to say "no" when things are not true for you, do not fit inside your value frame, are not in alignment with your purpose, or you just plain don't care to do it. When you say "no" to these things, you are clearing the path for the things that you do want. If our lives are so cluttered up with things we don't want or don't really care about, but we just do it because we feel obligated, then there is little to no room for what we do want.

Some people may have a poor reaction to you setting and holding your boundaries, especially if it's different than what you've been doing. Remember, you can't control other people's thoughts, feelings, or reactions. You can only control your response to them. What they think or feel or how they react is theirs to own.

To set or communicate a boundary, you can use this script as a guide:

"If you _____."

Fill in the blank with a very specific description of the person's behavior that you need to set a boundary around.

Example: "If you continue to stay out past the time we agreed upon," "I will _____."

Fill in the blank with the action you'll take if the boundary is violated. Your action is based on values and needs.

Example: "I will change your curfew to one hour earlier.
"If you still continue _____,
I will_____."

Fill in the blank with actions you'll take to make sure the boundary is followed.
Example: "If you still continue staying out past the agreed-upon time, I'll take away your car privileges."

Oftentimes when a boundary line is crossed, our emotions can get the better of us. When we try to communicate how something made us feel, we can easily fall into the blame game or the right/wrong game. A person's natural inclination is to defend herself when she's being made to feel wrong or attacked. This does not mean that you should stuff your feelings down and never express them. It means you need to give yourself time and space to feel whatever you're feeling without barfing it all over the other person.

Once you're able to ground yourself and have decided how you want to respond, keeping the results you want in mind, arrange to have a conversation with the person who crossed or pushed at your boundary. The best way I have found to do this successfully and not let my emotions rule the conversation is to use the Bradshaw Method.

You can use this script from the Bradshaw Method as a guide:

"When _____ happens."

Fill in the blank, describing the event. Be careful not to use accusatory language here.

Example: "When you do not come home at the agreed-upon time _____ happens, I feel_____."

Fill in the blank, describing how you feel. Remember to own your feelings. Do not use terms like, "You make me feel" or "You always/never."

Example: "I feel worried, scared, and disrespected."
"The result I want is_____."

Fill in the blank, describing the specific result that you desire.

Example: "The result I want is for our agreements to be kept and to not feel worried or scared for you like this."
"What I need from you is_____."
Or, "My request of you is_____."

Fill in the blank, stating what specific action you need from that person.

Example: "My request of you is that if something comes up where you are going to be later than we agreed upon, you'll call me to let me know."

Once you have made your specific request, ask to make a new agreement with the person. Now you have a new agreement. Remember, it is not fair, nor does it net you the results you want, when you hold past events over someone's head or save them up like stamps and then throw them in someone's face when it's something that has already been resolved.

CHAPTER 15

ZOMBIE BEFORE ZEN

In Chapter 10, I described the "mom zombie" mode I used to deal with my children when they were causing drama and I wanted to react to what they were doing. Going into zombie mode allowed me to respond in the appropriate way to achieve the results I wanted rather than just reacting, typically netting me negative results.

This doesn't just apply to moms; it can apply to any situation or relationship in your life that is in drama mode. When you choose, of your own volition, to live your life in conscious awareness and response versus reacting to whatever life throws your way, new possibilities open up. You'll be calm in the midst of chaos swirling around you.

We are all born with instinct—that fight-or-flight impulse that rises whenever we feel threatened emotionally or physically. People often react out of their first instinct—whatever it is. They may refer to this as "going with their gut." A gut reaction results in quick, unplanned, often thoughtless reactions—that "knee-jerk" response we sometimes regret. On the other hand, indecisiveness and non-reaction often causes us to freeze up.

Don't get me wrong. I'm not saying you should ignore your gut instinct. I'm saying listen deeper. Allow whatever first reaction comes up for you. Notice it. Take a breath. As you exhale that breath, envision how you want to respond to this situation. What would bring you the end result that you truly desire? Now choose your response. That brief pause may seem like a little thing, yet it can make all the difference in the world in the results you yield.

If you need more time than that brief pause, ask for it. A lot of people need more time to process what they are hearing, seeing, and feeling. I have found this to be true for me especially when it is an emotionally charged situation. I need extra time to sort out what is simply emotion, what is the root factor, and what is most often a fear-based emotion stemming from my limiting beliefs. I need time to clarify what the results are I truly want, and my purpose behind those results. Is my purpose to be right no matter what? Or is it one of my values or beliefs that is driving this emotion?

Why does it matter that you get control over your reactions in certain situations? For one very important reason: Those who continually react and don't take charge of their lives often turn into "drama" queens and kings—you know, the people who call you every day with a story about what "happened" to them, but never anything they could have done. They become the doormats for everybody to "hurt," "offend," "disappoint," or "humiliate," or generally wipe their feet on. Drama addicts turn their entire lives into a really bad soap opera. They perpetually live in "Victimville."

Those people who encase themselves in drama and always seem to be moving from one traumatic event to another avoiding what is really going on inside. Being continually caught up in the trauma or drama allows them to avoid looking in the mirror. They tend to get others caught or involved in the drama—and this gives them places to point blame. They also get to be right about themselves that nothing ever goes right for them because they are not good enough or whatever limiting belief they possess. Living in "Victimville" allows them to never be accountable for their choices. They are too caught up in the "woe is me" and sympathy received from others to bring in the results that would truly shift their lives. It's so easy to get caught up in the vicious cycle with them. To avoid this, you need to learn to respond rather than react.

How do you stop this vicious cycle? You choose your responses. This power of choice means that if it is someone else in your life who's in constant drama, rather than getting caught up in it with him or her, you ground yourself first. Then choose how you want to respond—from a calm and neutral place, you voice your position.

For example, if someone is acting emotionally about some drama that is happening in her life, instead of trying to fix it for her, ask her what you can do to best support her. A direct question often helps them to pause and figure out what they truly want and need.

If someone is ranting and raving at you, perhaps blaming you for what is happening in her life and attacking you personally, you can choose to not engage in the conversation. Instead, in a calm voice, state that you understand that she's upset and that you wish to help her through this, but you will not engage in the drama and personal attacks. Let her know that when she's ready to discuss it in a calm manner, with both parties fully listening, you'll be happy to do so. Ask her to let you know when she'll be ready to talk about it.

I understand that this may be difficult to do. It takes practice; lots of practice. When I experience this, I choose to step into what my kids call my "zombie role." I don't react. I get still and quiet. When they notice I'm not yelling back or reacting to what they're doing or saying, they tell me I'm being a zombie. I agree that I am, and state that I will remain so until they are willing to talk to me in a calm and reasonable manner, and to please let me know when that is.

They'll usually take some space, calm down, and then come talk with me. I've learned to not take accusations personally, which takes a lot of grounding and breathing. Instead, I ask questions. I'm accountable for choices I have made and things I have said. I ask the same of them. As I typically ask the questions, I find that what is going on has nothing to do with me. I'm just the easy target for their frustrations. This truth has played out in other relationships in my life, as well.

Before I understood this, I would get caught up in the drama, yell back, and make accusations of my own. This did not yield the results I wanted. Being able to step away from the drama, and not buy into it, keeps me from crumbling and falling down. Some events may knock me sideways, but I bounce back and keep moving.

This is all a part of being compassionate with yourself. It's too demanding to expect that once you have this knowledge and choose to live it, you'll respond they way you want without having to think about it. You will still have your instinct; a part of you will still want to immediately react. Once you've found that place of zen for yourself, events and people will seem to try to knock you out of it.

The bottom line is that if you find yourself knocked out of zen, step into zombie mode until you can properly choose your response that will net you the win-win results, and before you know it, you'll be right back into zen.

CHAPTER 16
SWEET SURRENDER

To be completely free and fully recovered from codependency, and move out of "Victimville" you must learn to forgive yourself and those who have hurt you in any way. Let go of your pain, anger, guilt, shame, and grief, and surrender to life and its crazy rollercoaster ride. This will enable you to fully embrace one of my favorite quotes:

> *"Life is not a journey to the grave with the intention of arriving safely in a pretty and well preserved body, but rather to skid in broadside, thoroughly used up, totally worn out, and loudly proclaiming—WOW—What a ride!"* - Unknown

Forgiveness
The word is easy to say, and yet the act can seem so difficult to do. Anyone can hold a grudge, but it takes a person with character and compassion to forgive. When you forgive, you release yourself from a painful burden. Forgiveness does not mean that you condone what happened or even that the person should be allowed back into your life. It means that you have made peace with the pain and are ready to let it go. You forgive other people because forgiving them helps you to heal yourself and move forward in your life. Forgiveness is an essential part to healing your past and all of your relationships.

I know it can seem unthinkable and even impossible to truly forgive the people in our lives who have hurt and wounded us the most, especially when it was someone that we loved and trusted. My grandfather was someone I loved and trusted, and he hurt me deeply. If I hadn't forgiven him, I would still be continually re-victimizing myself, and eventually this would have closed me off from loving myself and finding true love with Dave. I would have missed out on so much.

When you hold onto those negative emotions that person or past event brings up within you, it is like drinking poison and hoping your enemy will die. Those feelings are a toxin to your health and happiness. It will taint anything good that comes into your life, and you will be left wondering what went wrong and why you are back living in "Victimville" once again.

Most of us love to read stories about people who have responded to hatred with love. We find ourselves in awe and admiration that someone could be that generous of heart. Perhaps we even have a tiny bit of doubt that the person really felt the way they were responding. When we have been victimized, our initial reaction is typically anger, angst, shame, guilt, depression, righteousness, hatred, and so on. We have a hard time finding it within ourselves to respond to everything with love. Yet, study after study shows that one of the keys to longevity and good health is to develop a habit of gratitude, forgiveness, and letting go of past hurts.

Forgiveness isn't even about whether the person you are forgiving deserves it or not. It's really about you. What do you want? To be stuck in "Victimville," or even "Survivorhood," for the rest of your life? Or do you want to get the best revenge possible and live a long, happy life? If you choose the second option, then you must work on forgiving.

Here are some steps to help you forgive:

1. *Acknowledge*—Acknowledge what happened and how you felt at the time you were hurt. Look at the ways those same feelings show up in your life today and how it's affecting your ability to live a happy, successful life.

2. *Seek to understand*—Oftentimes understanding someone's motivation, problems, or sickness can help you to forgive and let go. Perhaps they were hurt the same way as a child and they have learned this behavior, or maybe they are trying to mask their own insecurities.

3. *Find the gratitude*—In every event, there is a learning opportunity. What did you learn from this event? Perhaps you discovered how to stand up for yourself or that you want to take someone's poor behavior as an example of what not to do. Make a list of the good things that emerged as a result of this awful experience. This will require you to look at the event from a completely new angle—the positive side. See if you can identify at least ten positive outcomes of this experience. Keep them somewhere where you can remind yourself of the positives when you're feeling negative.

4. *Be compassionate with yourself*—If you've ruminated over this problem for a long time, changing this pattern can take some time, too. You may find yourself slipping back into the old pattern from time to time. Don't beat yourself up over it; just acknowledge the slip and move on. Extreme emotional pain has a profound effect on the body. Allow yourself to mourn what could have been and then give yourself time to heal, physically and emotionally. Eat well. Rest. Focus on the natural beauty in the world. Give yourself permission to feel the emotions and process them. Don't bottle up the pain.

5. *Decide*—It's a sad fact that everyone is not trustworthy. Painful memories can serve to protect us from future hurts. It can enable you to see the same untrustworthy traits in other people who come into your life so you can use caution and possibly avoid getting hurt the same way. You get to decide whether or not that person should be in your life. If you choose to allow them in, take the time to carefully rebuild mutual trust. You can forgive someone without having any interaction with them. This option should be used if that person could cause you further harm or presents a danger.

6. *Karma*—Know that karma is a beautiful thing and takes care of itself. The only person whose karma you have control over is your own. Wishing bad things on people only serves to damage your own karma. If you can't bring yourself to love the person who hurt you, work on loving the learning opportunity they brought into your life.

7. *Visualize*—Use visualization techniques to aid in your forgiving and letting go.

    Example: Get in a quiet, calm place. Close your eyes and visualize the person standing in front of you. Know that he cannot harm you in any way. In this state, tell him everything you have ever wanted to tell him about how he hurt you, the effect the hurt had on your life, and fully express your anger, fear, and resentments. Once you are finished expressing yourself in this fashion, give him the opportunity to apologize for his actions. It's OK if he doesn't respond. Pause for a moment. Tell him you're now ready to forgive him, and let go of the negative ties that are binding you. Picture a cord that is tying you together. Now cut the cord, cauterize the ends, and allow him to leave your space.

    Another example: Get in a quiet, calm place. Close your eyes and visualize the person standing in front of you. Know the person can't harm you in any way. Surround him in a bubble of love. Usually this shows up as a pink bubble for me, but if yours is a different color, that's OK, too. Say, "I release you with love," and watch the person float away, surrounded in love.

How to Let Go

Letting go is a choice. It is telling yourself and the universe that you are taking charge and responsibility for your life. Letting go of what is no longer true for you or welcome in your life clears the path for better, brighter, and happier things to come in.

Here are some ways to help you let go:

1. *Clear out the clutter*—Get rid of anything that reminds you of that event or person, if it was a negative one. If you are trying to let go of someone you loved, I recommend picking one or two things that hold emotional value for you, and clearing out the rest.

2. *Write it out*—Write about the event or person in a journal or other safe place. Pour all your emotions and feelings into that paper. When it feels complete, stop.

3. *Have a releasing ceremony*—Take the pages that you wrote and burn them. Watch as the fire consumes your words, turning them to ash and releasing their energy out to the wind to be carried away.

If you choose not to write or are having a momentary fallback, find a rock and pour everything you're feeling into that rock, then hurl it as far away from you as you can, releasing it to the universe. Of course, always do this in a safe place where you won't break windows or hit someone with the rock.

How to Surrender and Move On

Surrendering reflects spiritual maturity and helps to fully free us from the bonds of codependency. It also requires patience and practice. In the end, it's worth it, as it allows us to enjoy our journey to an even fuller extent. Once I surrendered to life and gave up my illusion of control, things were no longer a struggle and life got easier. In fact, several times people have said to me, "It's so easy for you" when I've shared about letting go or dealing with obstacles. They're only seeing the results, not the journey I took to find this ease, and that's a good thing in my book. It reaffirms for me that I am on the right path.

Our source of suffering is always related to our resistance to what is. The soul doesn't try to control life; the ego does. Your ego is not a bad thing except when it's the only part of you that you're listening to. The ego is meant to protect you, and it's how we get things done. Unfortunately, our egos always think they know what's best for us and tend to drown out what our soul is saying. In protecting us, our ego tries to control the outcome in whatever we're doing. The key is to listen to both. Let your ego show you how to protect yourself, and move forward and listen to what your soul needs to be fulfilled and nourished. If you don't learn to surrender your will, you will surrender your peace.

It means letting go of how you think things should be and accepting them as they are. When we surrender, it doesn't mean we throw our hands in the air and do nothing; it means we pay close attention to our intuition so we can act on this wisdom. Then, once we've done what we can, we let go and allow grace to shine a light on a better path—one that brings about the result that ultimately serves our highest good. In other words, don't get so caught up in how you think the result should come to you or look. Declare what you want and take action toward making it happen. Leave the "when" and "how" it shows up to the universe. You'll be pleasantly surprised at the outcome.

I believe there are some things in life that are going to happen no matter what you say or do, and other things that happen because of choices we make. The thing is we don't get to know which is which, so we have to make the best choices possible with the knowledge that we have.

Sometimes the "why" of things is revealed to us, and sometimes it's not, like after my dad had his stroke and was in a long-term care facility. His dementia caused him to act completely out of character at times, and he was sometimes violent.

One day, he rolled over the foot of an RN with his wheelchair on purpose because she wouldn't let him have a cookie right then. She went to the doctor, as she thought her foot was broken. While they were running tests on her, they discovered cancer in its early stages. She was able to be treated and the cancer was removed.

She later called my mom to thank her for my dad rolling over her foot. My mom had been feeling extremely guilty over the incident. She said that if he hadn't done that, she wouldn't have gone to the doctor and they wouldn't have caught the cancer in time.

Surrendering is not the same as giving up. Please don't confuse the two. Surrendering in this way can take monumental strength. Giving up isn't even in the same category.

The difference between Surrendering and Giving Up

1. Surrender keeps you connected. It may involve painful decisions, but you can still feel a sense of peace and a

A Hot Mess

connection with your truth. Giving up feels shallow, reactive, or incomplete inside.

2. Surrender is a decision. When you surrender, you remain engaged. You step in and choose your role in a situation. Giving up is not so much a decision as a way out.

3. Surrender is drama-free. Giving up nearly always involves dramatic exasperation and blame on outside people or circumstances. Surrender needs no fanfare. It makes itself known only through its undeniable clarity.

4. Surrender means consciously choosing to let go.

CHAPTER 17

LEARNING HEALTHY LOVE

Most of us were raised to put others first—always. As a result, we have a society that is primarily codependent and unhealthy physically, mentally, and emotionally. When you always put others first and leave yourself out, you're being **Exclusive**. The next generation appears to be trying to shift from this, and often has gone to the other extreme. By always putting themselves first, they end up acting entitled, feeling unhappy, and are not sure why. When you always put yourself first, you are being **Reclusive**.

In order to live a happier, healthier, successful life, you need to strive to be **Inclusive**. This is where you live holding the "and," giving to yourself *and* others. This way no one is left out. You are just as deserving of your time, gifts, and love as everyone around you.

So how do you know when to put yourself first and when to put others first? If you're constantly giving to others without replenishing and re-energizing yourself, you'll soon burn out, thereby cheating everyone of your gifts.

Picture your energetic reserve like a gas tank. The gas is energy; this is what you expend when you give to others. When you give to yourself first, you "top off" your tank. If you're constantly running on just above empty, you are always on edge, stressed, and in imminent danger of running out of gas. If a detour— meaning an unplanned event or chaos— crops up, your stress level raises, and you may find yourself delayed as you sit by the road waiting for someone to help you. If you continually top yourself off, the detours will not be as stressful and you will not have the added stress of becoming depleted, waiting for someone else to help you out. You will always have the energy (fuel) needed to give to others and live in service when you live in this practice.

Practicing being *inclusive* in your life helps to bring you into balance. Life balance is not a mathematical equation. It is not 20% here, 20% there. Balance for each person may look different. The key is finding out what living a life of balance looks like for you, and then taking action on it.

A codependent person who is still stuck in the day-to-day mire of living to be needed is typically so far out of balance that she's not cognizant of what she can do to bring herself into balance. But can codependent people achieve life balance if they bring the issue to the forefront?

Yes! And perhaps with this focus in mind, it may be easier for them to shift from being codependent to living a happy and fulfilling life.

Let's start with one of the most common symptoms of a codependent person: the constant need to fix or rescue others. Remember, we discussed this in Chapter 13. This will help you move out of the drama triangle and into the thrive triangle. As long as you are going from person to person in your life, and reacting to their events, it takes the focus off of you and your own life. It's a great avoidance tool.

What would happen if you put the focus squarely on you for once? What would you find?

This can be scary ground for someone who has never done it, or hasn't done it in a long time. If you feel the need to create a safety net for yourself in order to start, make this agreement with yourself. Right now, you're only exploring. You're not committing to anything, nor do you need to change anything. Just be open and willing to explore the possibilities.

That's right—it's an adventure. Take it as such. Play with it, have fun with it, challenge yourself, and stretch your abilities. Get out some paper and a pen and answer the following question. If it was mandatory that you take a minimum of one to four hours a week and spend it doing something for yourself that did not involve serving or taking care of others, what would you be doing? Time and money are not in the equation here.

How would you feel when you were doing it? How about afterwards? Who would be there? Where would you be? What smells are around you? What tastes? If someone were to look at you, what would she see?

Write out as many different things as you can think of. Put in as much detail as possible. Don't second guess or limit what you write. Just put it down, no matter how silly or unrealistic it may seem to you right now. Remember—you're just exploring. Keep adding to the list as things come to you.

Now pick one or two items from your list that you can begin to schedule into your life this week. Put it on your calendar and honor it. Try to stick to it as much as you would as if it was a meeting with someone else who you had made a commitment with.

Do that one thing for you for one week, noticing while you're doing it how you feel, what your energy level is, how others are responding to you. At the end of the week, decide if these items are something you want to commit to for another week, or maybe you want to try two different ones. Whichever direction it is, schedule in the time.

There are times when the line is not so clear between giving to yourself and giving to others. This is often when a team is involved in something. Decisions you make can often affect the entire team. So who do you put first? Do you do what's best for you, or what's best for everyone else?

For best results, when working with a team, look at and evaluate the following:

1. What would I do if I put myself first? What would the results potentially be? How will I feel? What are the benefits? What are the downfalls? Who would gain the most?

2. What would I do if I put others first? What would the results potentially be? How would I feel? What are the benefits? What are the downfalls? Who would gain the most?

3. Always look for the win/win approach. Talk to the rest of your team. Evaluate their feedback along with your own. Is there a way that will benefit all? This is often a combination or compromise of your answers to number one and number two.

Guilt

As you begin to transform yourself from being a hot mess into a happy success, people around you may try to resist your changes. They are used to you being one way, and even though change is the only true constant in life, most people resist it. Some of them may even try to use the guilt card with you. Being the hot mess you were, it probably worked pretty well on you in the past.

Wikipedia states that guilt is a cognitive or an emotional experience that occurs when a person realizes or believes—accurately or not—that he has violated a moral standard and is responsible for that violation. It is closely related to the concept of remorse.

What purpose does guilt serve for you? In my research, I came across people who believe that guilt is a good thing; that it is our moral compass and keeps us on the straight and narrow. While I do believe this is true to some degree, I also believe that many people have abused it by using it for manipulation to serve their own purposes.

I recently heard a motivational speaker state that women make their decisions from their guilt. I'm sure there are a few men who fit into this category also, but I can see where women may tend to do this more frequently. Women are typically ruled by their emotions, and if guilt is a constant in their life, it will influence their decisions heavily. Living this way will keep you firmly planted in "Victimville."

Guilt may also be used as a mechanism to allow those people to temporarily feel good about themselves. They feel good about themselves because they feel bad about what they're doing, so that must mean they are basically good—kind of twisted logic, but there it is. This occurs while making no concerted effort to change what they're doing. For example, a thief can feel he's basically a good person deep down inside, even while living outside of his own moral values. After all, some thieves do feel bad about what they are doing, just not bad enough to do something different.

Guilt is fed from our own self-limiting beliefs. When parents use guilt to try to get a child to do something their way, they are enforcing that belief—whether they intend to do that or not. When a spouse asks why you need to go get a pedicure when you should be spending time with them and/or the children, what is it that you really hear in your head? "I'm not a good mother," "I'm not a good wife," and "I'm not good enough."

On some level you may believe this about yourself, so when someone pushes that button, you immediately feel guilt and begin to question your decisions. Guilt lets a simple decision/result moment last a whole lot longer so a person can wallow in it more. Society, and usually our parents, tell us that we are not to be selfish, and to put others first. We spend most of our time trying to please our parents, and everyone else, with how selfless we are. Selflessness does not equal *not* being selfish. Being selfless means that you are being yourself less. That's not what this world needs. We need more of you. Only when you are authentically standing in your own power being fully *you* will others truly benefit.

What to do to stop living in guilt

1. If you actually made a choice that did not have the end result you wanted, be accountable for your choice and make a new agreement with that person that will bring about the results you want. If the person chooses to not respond to you or continues to harp on it, know that you can only be accountable for your choices and can only control your responses.

2. Realize that no one is perfect. Ask others about their issues and listen to their answers and imperfections.

3. There's a lesson, whether we want to see it or not, in every event. Look for the lesson and move on. It may be as simple as a reminder that you don't want to be that way to others. It doesn't have to be a huge, deep, Dalai Lama lesson. Just absorb the learning and keep moving.

4. Recognize what is underneath your guilt, and work on that self-limiting belief. Put personal practices into place that will help shift you from that belief into a positive, empowering one. Affirming mantras are a good place to start.

5. Don't get sucked in when someone tries to guilt-trip you. When someone begins what you perceive to be a guilt trip, nip it in the bud. State firmly that you appreciate their view and you will take their opinion into consideration while you make what you believe to be the best decision for your life, or just firmly state what your decision

is and move on to a new topic. If they are still not getting it and continue to try the guilt trip, it may be time to put it on the table.

Don't play the blame game. State what is going on and how you feel. Use the Bradshaw Method I described in Chapter 14. Be sure to state what you request to be changed in the future, and get an agreement from the other person.

Remember, when you are your authentic self, you are living a fulfilled, balanced life, which translates to being able to give more to others. People benefit just from being around you. Many studies have been done that show that happiness is contagious. Fill your tank first, then give to others from that abundant place. You will find that you have no room for guilt or regrets.

Healthy Giving

Another common trait among codependents is carrying other people's emotional or "energetic" baggage. We tend to take the world on our shoulders and then wonder why our muscles are so tight. We walk around wearing our shoulders for earrings. Do you wonder why you can help others so well, but can't seem to help yourself? Do you literally feel the pain that other people are experiencing?

If these questions and statements resonate with you, then—.

Put those bags down! They're not yours!

This is an extension of the Rescue Ranger problem discussed in Chapter 13, and it intertwines with not taking care of yourself. We take on others' energetic baggage without even realizing it in most cases.

Drawing from my own experience, I know this to be true. I was always helping others, listening, coaching, advising, empathizing, and I would eventually find myself drained, energetically depleted, or depressed for seemingly no reason. Never one to give up, I'd keep going until I crashed. I'd often be "crashed" for three to four days, holed up in bed, on the couch, ignoring the phone, the door, and the mail. I called these crashes "funks." I avoided all contact as much as possible during a crash. My family and friends learned to tiptoe around me during those times.

During my funks, I'd let out all of the dark, negative, victim thoughts until I was empty. To bring myself back up into the land of the living, I would slowly start feeding myself positive reinforcements.

This pattern impacted my relationships with my family, friends, and my job. Tired of living this pattern and realizing it needed to change as I recovered from my codependency, I created my GIVER Method™ to keep me from carrying others' "energetic" baggage, allowing me to give in a healthy way.

GIVER Method™

1. **G—*Ground myself*.** I start and end each day and process with grounding myself. I also ground whenever a stressful situation arises. Grounding is connecting your mind, body, and spirit to each other and then to the earth and the Divine.

2. **I—*Intention*.** After grounding I set my intention for the day or process. If I am giving someone healing, I start with and chant my intention statement for that process. This keeps me focused on the end result I am seeking and keeps my "stuff" from mixing with theirs. An example of an intention statement is, "I send this healing energy where it is needed. I will not take away from the lesson that needs to be learned here. I leave what is necessary and send what is not back to Mother Earth. I do no harm. I send and receive love." I chant this mantra out loud or in my head throughout the process.

3. **V—*Visualize*.** I visualize what is being released from the person. I see it in my mind as it travels out of them and either directly into the earth, my first choice, or passes through me. I concentrate on being a channel and not hanging onto anything, sending it into the earth. I visualize them as being healed and healthy.

4. **E—*Evaluate and Expel*.** I do a check-in with myself during and after the process. I will take an internal inventory of thoughts and feelings and evaluate what is truly my 'baggage' and what is not. Anything that is not mine, or just plain needs to be released, gets expelled. I

visualize it, and it usually looks like black crud to me, coming out of my chakras and down into the earth where it becomes fertilizer that helps me continue to grow. I continue expelling until I sense that it is gone.

5. **R -*Replenish***. I then replenish myself by drawing bright healing light from the earth and the Divine. I continue to cycle it throughout my body, mind, and spirit until I feel re-energized. I close with gratitude for the gift of a never-ending supply of energy and love.

I created the GIVER Method™ as I learned that taking on and carrying other people's energetic baggage was actually robbing them of a lesson they were meant to learn. That was like saying they weren't capable of carrying their own baggage and deciding on their own when to release it. Through my journey, I have learned to hold each person as whole, complete, and capable. I do this with compassion, faith, and love. I always practice being a GIVER. I encourage you to try the GIVER Method™ and share your experience with me.

CHAPTER 18

GET YOUR REVENGE!

Now is your moment. You get to decide. What are you going to do with all of this information I just shared with you? Since you've read the book this far. I have to believe it resonated with you on some level. Perhaps you found the parallels in your life stories as you read mine. I do hope you didn't have to experience everything I did, but whether you did or not, know that every experience held value and served a purpose. I challenge you to start taking the exercises and practices I shared with you and implementing them into your day-to-day life. Chances are you've heard bits and pieces of them before but never really applied them to your life, or maybe you didn't even believe you could. Now is the time to do something different. Trust yourself.

Making changes in your life can bring up a lot of fear, especially when you're stepping into unknown territory. People deal with fear in different ways. Some try to ignore it and just surge forward anyway, while others dwell on unknown territory and let it control their decisions. There's another option when fear shows up for me. I remind myself what fear really is—False Expectations Appearing Real.

The things I'm afraid of haven't happened yet; therefore, they are an expectation—not reality. I've also learned that if I focus on False Expectations Appearing Real long enough, eventually, reality can overcome them. For example, when I was so afraid of my romantic partner leaving me, I tried to become who I thought he wanted, rather than who I really was. That's why he ended up leaving me. So if I don't want it to happen, that means I need to turn my focus on what I do want, rather than what I don't.

I've had people tell me they envy me, admire me, or that they just plain don't believe that I understand how hard it is for them to make the changes I've shared here, because it seems so easy and effortless for me. I worked hard to get to this point until I realized that it doesn't have to be hard. I was just making it that way. I was really good at getting in my own way and sabotaging myself. I didn't want to live that way anymore, so I chose to be really good at defining and holding my boundaries, forgiveness and gratitude, letting go and surrendering, and compassionately loving unconditionally.

It's that simple. Right there, that moment that you choose to live that way, that's the magical moment that transformation begins. To keep it moving forward, you must have a clear vision, believe in yourself and that vision, and take action to make it happen. The first step is to get clear about what your definition is of what a happy, successful life looks like for you. When you picture yourself as successful, what do you see? I recommend writing a clear description of this vision or draw, paint, or sculpt it, something that you can refer back to when you want to remind yourself of the end result you want and what it looks like. Picture it. Immerse yourself in it until you can feel it physically in your body. Now memorialize that feeling in some way so that you will recognize it when you feel it again. You'll want to measure your results based on those feelings rather than the picture, because chances are it won't look like what you thought. It will be better.

The second step is to believe in your success. Successes can be small or big. Celebrate and acknowledge each one. You will have your big overall success with accomplishments along the way that are action steps toward your dream of success. Acknowledging each success is important and helps to guard against the feelings of impossibility, inertia, and apoptosis, meaning the feeling of being no longer needed. Can you believe in your dream no matter what obstacles come into your path? When your faith wavers, what do you do?

Do you take obstacles as signs that you're on the wrong path, or do you work to strategize around them? Determine if the perceived obstacle is based on a limited belief about yourself or if it's based on the need for a strategy.

It's my belief that you can choose to create a new empowering belief instead. It helps to anchor this by also creating a personal practice that you can use when you catch yourself falling back into the old belief, or to bolster the new empowering belief. For example, a person's limiting belief is that she is not good enough. Her new empowering belief is that she is strong and capable. The practice to anchor this is that each morning she looks in the mirror, flexes her muscles, and says out loud, "I am strong and capable in all ways." She does this until she believes it, and as needed when the limiting belief crops up. It may sound simple, but the changes this process can bring are simply amazing.

If you find that you are struggling to believe it and it feels like you're lying to yourself when you state your empowering belief, take a small step back. Make it a progressive empowering statement instead. Try, "I am working toward being strong and capable in all ways."

If it is an obstacle that needs strategy, there are many different avenues to take. You can brainstorm around it. You can engineer it out. You can gather your dream team and utilize their resources, thoughts, and ideas, or ask them to support you by telling you if they observe you starting to slip into your old patterns. Reach out. No one was meant to travel this journey alone. Most people enjoy helping others reach their dream. Make it easy for them to say, "Yes!" Be specific in your request of them. Let them know exactly what you need and by when. I firmly believe there is a way over, under, around, or through any obstacle.

Step number three is to take action. Make movement toward manifesting your dream life. Focus on what you want, rather than what you don't. Look at what your reality is now, and your dream of what you want to manifest. Strategize action steps toward your dream. For example, if your dream is to be a wildly successful coach, write down all you believe is required to accomplish being that dream, such as an awesome logo, business cards, flyers, networking, a business plan, professional liability insurance, paying clients, a great niche. You get the idea. You can brainstorm with others on what they think it will take. Interview some wildly successful coaches. Research your dream. What have others done to get there? Would you do the same, or different than they did?

Now organize all of those goals into categories, such as marketing, your business set up, marketing, and networking. Once your goals are in a category, you can prioritize them so that you're not trying to do it all at once. By trying to do too much at once, it's easy to get overwhelmed that way and give yourself an excuse to give up on your dream. Check off your goals and celebrate each goal you accomplish. I call this process "chunking it down." You chunk the goals off into smaller, easily achievable bites, and each goal will flow much easier. I'm sure you've heard the saying, "How do you eat an elephant? One bite at a time." I like to take that saying a step further and say, "Sometimes you have to put some of the elephant in the freezer so that it doesn't go bad." Have your overall larger goals, but have your smaller goals that move you toward them. Don't give yourself impossible deadlines. Be compassionate with yourself, and celebrate your successes along the way.

If you truly want success in your life, you can manifest it.

As Glinda the Good Witch said to Dorothy in the Wizard of Oz, "You've always had the power, my dear. You just had to learn it for yourself."

You can use this easy method for accomplishing goals and transforming your life. If you don't like the results you get, remember there is no playing the blame game or beating yourself up. It simply means those results are not working for you, so you get to make a new choice.

Living life this way takes practice, so be compassionate with yourself and be sure to celebrate your successes.

I want to leave you with one last statement that a friend shared with me on Facebook. I don't know who the original author is, but it summed up so well what I want for you that I have to include it.

> *"Give, but don't allow yourself to be used. Love, but don't allow your heart to be abused. Trust, but don't be naive. Listen to others, but don't lose your own voice." - Unknown*

Get your own revenge—be happy!

END

AUTHOR'S NOTE

This story is a work of fiction compiled from interviews and research from various sources. I chose to write it as if told from a single person, sharing the tragedies of their lives and what they learned from them. I've shared with as much transparency as possible, and not with the intent of making anyone appear as a bad person, but only with the intent to share how my character's interaction with them and her choices around or about them affected her results.

My purpose in sharing this story and what I have learned on this crazy rollercoaster of life is to help others who are struggling and feeling stuck in "Victimville," or are merely surviving in "Survivorhood," to move into "Thrive Town" with me. Nothing gives me greater joy than seeing people empower themselves, find that spark of magic within themselves, and become thriving, happy, successful beings. If I have helped anyone in any way do this, then I have served my purpose.

I am loving my life in "Thrive Town" and screaming "Whooohooo!" at the top of my lungs throughout all the ups, downs, and crazy turns.

> *"Life is not a journey to the grave with the intention of arriving safely in a pretty and well preserved body, but rather to skid in broadside, thoroughly used up, totally worn out, and loudly proclaiming—WOW—What a Ride!"*   - Unknown

I hope you'll join me.

RESOURCES

1. "Codependent No More," Melody Beattie
   http://melodybeattie.com
2. "Men Are from Mars and Women Are from Venus" John Gray, Ph.D.
   http://www.marsvenus.com
3. Codependents Anonymous
   http://www.coda.org
4. "Your Power Source Tap™—The Easy Way to Be Grounded," Bo Bradley
   https://www.smashwords.com/books/view/69911
5. "Achieving the Balance Dream—11 Secrets to Living a Life of Balance," Bo Bradley
   www.bobradley.blogspot.com